# ONE MORE "LOST PEACE"?

## Rethinking the Cold War after Twenty Years

Edited by
**Raffaele D'Agata**
**Lawrence Gray**

**University Press of America,® Inc.**
Lanham · Boulder · New York · Toronto · Plymouth, UK

**Copyright © 2011 by**
**University Press of America,® Inc.**
4501 Forbes Boulevard
Suite 200
Lanham, Maryland 20706
UPA Acquisitions Department (301) 459-3366

Estover Road
Plymouth PL6 7PY
United Kingdom

Library of Congress Control Number: 2010936061
ISBN: 978-0-7618-5394-7 (clothbound : alk. paper)
ISBN: 978-0-7618-5395-4 (paperback : alk. paper)
eISBN: 978-0-7618-5396-1

Published with the contribution of Università di Sassari,
Dipartimento di Storia
John Cabot University, Rome

Cover Image: Vedran Smailović playing the cello in the
partially destroyed National Library of Sarajevo in 1992.
Photo by Mikhail Evstafiev.
Licensed under the Creative Commons
Attribution ShareAlike license, version 2.5.

™
⊖⊖ The paper used in this publication meets the minimum
requirements of American National Standard for Information
Sciences—Permanence of Paper for Printed Library Materials,
ANSI Z39.48-1992

# Contents

# Preface

The genesis for this book was a seminar held in 2008 in Sassari, Sardinia, a town known as the birthplace of a disproportionate number of Italian statesmen in the postwar era. The seminar brought together two old friends, who had known one another nearly forty years ago. An Italian and an American: scholars in their thirties then, they were excited by the heady political and intellectual atmosphere of Italy in the 70's and early 80's. Both had participated in political movements in their respective countries, and both were investigating what the Cold War was actually about and why it was preventing social progress, and how that could be changed.

Now here we are with everything altered, but not in the way we had expected or hoped. Twenty years after the Cold War ended we wanted to revisit the issues which loomed so large then, when a happier ending—with no winners and no losers—seemed possible.

The seminar in Sassari offered an opportunity to re-examine those missed chances and assess their credibility by inviting scholars to share their views on this provocative topic, that is, the possible "lost peace". Since 2008 there have been some important works on the Cold War, including the 3 volume Cambridge History. In fact, the participants in this book include one co-editor and several contributors to that important work.

We wish to thank Jackie Quillen for her assistance with the editing, and the Department of History of the University of Sassari and John Cabot University of Rome for the publication of this book.

.

*Rome, July 2010*

Raffaele D'Agata
Lawrence Gray

# Introduction

Why should we raise the question that makes for the title of this book? As a matter of fact, we basically all know that the Cold War did end much more smoothly, and—above all—much more peacefully, than was threatened through the nuclear arms race. Thus far, there were no real losers. Everybody seems to be a winner. Moreover, as early as 1989, while several heavy constraints were lifted from the lives of millions of East Europeans, and the end of the Berlin wall occurred, hope became the keyword to describe the process.

Yet, on the other hand, what followed was not properly any actual blessing to several million people who lived in the former communist countries. For them, the transition from the Soviet system into some kind of market society carried with it an increase of economic insecurity. Increasing violence appeared to be associated with this transition, including high-intensity warfare in the Balkan peninsula, the bombing of the Russian Parliament, and warfare and terror inside the Russian Federation. This outcome was just the opposite of what the defeated European countries had experienced after the Second World War, that is, the positive result of more than two decades of increasing welfare and justice. Clearly, some opportunities were lost. The two decades that have elapsed since the end of the Cold War have not been more peaceful than the previous years. Inside Europe—witness the Balkans—peace has not ensued.

How should we try to explain this? Why did the "victory" of the West not lead to peace? Possibly the reasons for this have much to do with why the present degree of economic insecurity throughout the world is greater now than at any other time since 1929. Some contributions to this book either suggest or try to demonstrate that the present situation has much to do with how the Cold War actually ended—or, rather, with how it started to end significantly more than just twenty years ago. One idea that has been tested and debated during the symposium which gave origin to this book is that the kind of "West" that finally won the Cold War was not the same kind of "West" that had started it.

The original call for the papers now included in this book was inspired by the basic assumption that the two decades following the end of the Cold War may be seen as strikingly similar to the decades which followed World War I, with respect to both the economy and political stability. Accordingly, it is also assumed that the Cold War itself may be seen as analogous to World War I under many aspects, including the doubts about who was responsible for its outbreak and the fundamental uselessness of its sacrifices.

Similarities between the Cold War and World War I may be noticed both in terms of the structure of the international system and in terms of some key words affecting public debate, propaganda, and mobilization. Between 1989 and 1991, as after 1918, at least one mighty empire was disintegrated. And, like immediately after 1918, a victory in the name of democracy was officially claimed just while a substantial stream of democratic thinking—from several different approaches—found a lot of reasons to feel increasingly doubtful and disappointed. Furthermore, in both cases, some nasty and bloody nationalisms were unleashed out of a malicious evolution of often respectable national claims.

As relates to economics, similarities may appear less evident at first glance —at least, as far as some current commonplaces are accepted. It is widely assumed that the breakdown of the Soviet system gave way to a worldwide success of capitalist market rules. In fact capitalism was undergoing some severe challenges after World War I—as represented by the early momentum of the Soviet revolution and, later, by the forms of administered and controlled economy that were developed by the Fascist regimes. Yet, a deeper insight reveals that the present dominance of classical market rules on a world scale is not less presumptive, nor less ideologically manipulated, than during the 1920s and the 1930s. Imperial power politics, and the related monetary and financial artifices, were determinant factors of the precarious balance of world capitalism between the two world wars. Witness the strident contrast between the optimistic rhetoric of globalization and the epidemics of virulent warfare that has raged so wildly throughout the world during the 1990s and the early 2000s.

Those contradictions may be related to a basic pattern that is shared by both the post-bipolar system and the Versailles system: that is, the dominant power status of one nation, which is not supported by any corresponding soundness of its economic situation—as was the case of Britain about 1930, and of the United States about 2000. Moreover, the United States became much more vulnerable, even in terms of its security at home, after the disappearance of its supposed arch-enemy in the Cold War. Indeed, one could hypothesize that the way "victory" in the Cold war was pursued, how much it cost, and what kind of entanglements it involved, led to the climate that allowed 9/11 to happen.

So, finally, are there people who can credibly claim to have won the Cold War? If anyone can make that claim, it ought to be people who were not familiar with its long term aims. The overwhelming majority of mankind—including most people in the US today—is being left with a huge bill to pay. Whoever actually won the Cold War did reach that goal through means that are fundamentally alien to democratic values. Those means are the pursuit of deregulation of world financial markets, the benign neglect of illegal business in the field of drugs and weapons, the increase in the scope and use of "covert"—i.e. unavowable—political and military actions, and the enlistment as partners those who fought Soviet communism because of the ideas it theoretically shared with democratic thinking more than because those ideas were largely misinterpreted by Soviet ideology and behavior. The question is: was "victory" in the Cold War the result of "accidental" practices of the "winners", or due to identifiable steps that were part of a strategic process?

It could be said that something else was at stake in the Cold War. Intellectual ideas and moral forces also confronted each other about what democracy should mean and how human welfare should be pursued. Many people honestly thought that this was precisely what was at stake. A question that recurs often in the pages that follow is whether the outcome would have been very different had these concerns actually been given careful scrutiny.

# SECTION I

# WHAT WAS AT STAKE FOR THE "LOSERS"?

*Wilfried Loth*

# Soviet Ambivalences, Western Overstatements

The "events of 1989" changed the study of the Cold War in two ways. While historians previously studied a period of contemporary history with an unknown outcome, they have been dealing with a closed subject since 1989. It is roughly known how this story ended. This allows for a more precise approach to the subject, a more precise definition of the terms, and a more astute weighing of the factors. On the other hand, the opening up of archives in the former sphere of influence of the Soviet Empire has reduced the previous one-sidedness of the approach to the sources of history of the Cold War: Even if much source material still is not available, it has become possible in principle to study decision-making processes in the Soviet sphere of influence.[1]

My paper develops from the availability of internal sources of the Eastern side, which has become possible after the breakdown of the "Soviet empire". How did it expand our notion of the Cold War, the knowledge of its context and developments? So far these archives have been analyzed selectively, they are only partially accessible, and some, such as party- and government documents of the Soviet Union, have now been closed once again. Accordingly, many specific questions still have not been answered.[2] A picture emerges that does not fundamentally alter the knowledge we had of the period before the opening up of Eastern archives, but which presents the Eastern side in a more colorful and more vivid light, and which in some regards has brought out new features.[3]

## Stalin's Ambivalences

During the Cold War, cooperation and confrontation were closely interlinked. The one could always turn into the other, "hawks" (hardliners) could always turn into "doves" and vice versa. This already applies to Stalin and the beginning of the Cold War. Archival sources impressively confirm Stalin's paranoia and total restlessness: at the same time, however, it has become clear that his interest in the continuation of cooperation with the Western powers was even stronger and more persistent than was believed before.

In this manner, the first and most comprehensive war objectives program of the Moscow leadership, edited by Ivan Maisky, the chairman of the Commission for the Planning for Reparations to be Extracted from the Defeated Enemy States, and handed to Foreign Minister Vyacheslav Molotov on January 11th 1944, considered the "strengthening of friendly relations with the USA and Britain" to be the first element of post-war politics. Here, Maisky primarily focused on Great Britain, which he saw in a conflict of interest with the USA and he intended to "utilize as a counterbalance to the imperialist expansion of the USA." Regarding the internal order of the countries of freed Europe, he stated it was to "be based on the principles of a broad democracy, in the spirit of the notions of the popular front." The Allies were to cooperate in the realization of this objective: There are reasons to assume that regarding the democratization of the regimes in post-war Europe it will be possible for the USSR, the USA and Britain to cooperate, even if it is not always going to be easy."[4]

The installation of Communist hegemony in Eastern Europe thus either appears to be the result of a power political confrontation with anti-Soviet forces—such as Poland, Bulgaria and Rumania—or the product of the interaction of national revolutionaries and Soviet controllers, who were not up to the task of democratization, and, therefore, adopted the Soviet model—such as in the Soviet zone of occupation in Germany and in Hungary.[5] Yet, even the national party leadership included politicians who did not interpret the "democratic way to Socialism" merely as a temporarily necessitated tactical approach—such as Wladislaw Gomulka, who imposed a democratic program on the Polish Workers' Party in December 1945, or Imre Nagy in Hungary. It was only in 1947/48 that the old style party dogmatists were able to finally push through, when Stalin developed a pathological fear of "counterrevolutionary" actions of the "imperialists" and their allies in the "people's democratic" countries.[6]

The dogmatic toughening of 1947/48, however, should not be equated with a complete rejection of cooperation with the Western powers. As the correspondence between Andrei Shdanov and Stalin in the Fall of 1947 shows, they really interpreted the conditions in Moscow the way they argued publicly: not only did Stalin really believe in the "subjugation" of the European countries to American imperialism; he also seriously hoped that the Communists would be able to mobilize the majority of the democratic and national forces against the Marshall-Plan and Western bloc-building. The thesis that "two camps" had formed in international politics did not mean—as has been gathered in view of later events—that the Soviet leadership now turned to the confrontation of the Eastern and the Western bloc. Rather, Stalin saw "two opposing lines in international politics."

The victory of the "anti-imperialist and democratic line" in the West was to make it possible to continue with cooperation in the interest of securing the peace and of preventing the permanent division of Europe.[7]

However, the means Stalin applied indeed had the opposite effect: a "general strike" and "militant workers' demonstrations" were by no means likely to win the "struggle for return of the Communists to the government" (as Shdanov told the Italian CP top leader Luigi Longo[8]) in Western Europe, and by closing its own ranks the division between the East and the West grew. Both at the same time further increased the ever latent Western fear of aggressive Soviet Communism. This also increased the gap between intention and effect in Stalinist policies. The Soviet dictator more and more acted within a world of imaginary dangers and chances; the ideologically blurred perception of reality made it impossible to influence the actual course of events outside his sphere of power.[9] Regarding the Soviet side, therefore, ideologically based misperceptions of Western policies are one cause for the failure of East-West cooperation. The others are controlling weaknesses of a system, in which the Soviet ruler wanted to decide everything himself, but presumably was told by his informants only what he wanted to hear.

Thus, clearly, the Soviet interest in cooperation with the Western powers was even stronger than has previously been gathered. In the pursuit of his security and great power interests, Stalin deferred the export of the Bolshevist revolution even further. He had an even more pragmatic approach to the development of the scenarios on Eastern Europe. Stalin was obviously more constructive in his thoughts on East Germany; clinging more tightly to the perspective of cooperation than should be assumed in light of the aggressive propaganda terminology in the Cominform style. On the other hand, the ideological limits of his ability to cooperate as well as those that were necessitated by the system have become clearer: the exaggerated fears and the illusions concerning political decision-making processes in the West, the inability to appropriate information input, to trust-building diplomacy, and to the realization of democratization programs for which the Soviet Union was responsible as an occupation power. In view of these weaknesses of the Stalinist system, Communist movements and class-struggle ideology were able to win their own momentum within the sphere of power of the Red Army, which objectively were not in line with the strategic objectives of the Soviet dictator.[10]

Stalin's successors were more realistic in their perception of Soviet interests and Western politics, yet they were subjected to pressures of the Communist bureaucracies, the interests of which amounted to little more than the extension of their own power and the basic conservation of the existing system of rule. It was this pressure, and the perception of the aggressiveness of Western policies, which were responsible for the decision to intervene in Hungary in 1956.


## Coping with the Heritage

It took Nikita Khrushchev one week to decide if a solution with the reform communist Imre Nagy could be found. He only decided in favor of the "military path" after Mao Zedong and Palmiro Togliatti had voted accordingly. Next to his concern for his position as leader of the CPSU and World Communism, apparently, the continuous fear of Western imperialists played a role. "If we leave Hungary", he reasoned in the party executive committee, "it will give great impetus to the Americans, the British and the French—to the imperialists. They will consider it a weakness on our side and move into the offensive [...] They will then add Hungary to Egypt."[11]

The pressure that motivated Khrushchev's risky Berlin Ultimatum had similar origins: the continuous wave of refugees from the GDR and the preparations for the nuclear rearmament of the Federal Republic made him look like a loser in the eyes of potential competitors. The threat to transfer the control of transition routes from West Berlin to the GDR at least promised to force the acceptance of the GDR. It might also prevent the stationing of nuclear weapons in the Federal Republic and remove the threat imposed by West Berlin. "It is our primary objective", he explained his endeavor to Foreign Minister Andrei Gromyko and his staff, "to squeeze them out of Berlin like a disgusting pimple from the nose. This is our maximum program, so to speak; but it should not be that easy to be realized. But we can wring out the recognition of the GDR from them and solve the German question on this basis. Then there will be two German states [...] and, of course, without nuclear or other modern weapons. This is our minimum program."[12]

With the stationing of the Soviet nuclear weapons in Cuba, Kruschev on the one hand intended to compensate for the drastic superiority of the USA in nuclear armaments, which Deputy Defense Minister Roswell Gilpatric had now even made public in a speech delivered in October 1961. On the other hand, he wanted to prevent another American invasion of the sugar island, which threatened to damage his prestige as leader of the Communist world. The Americans, he later complained in his memoirs, "had surrounded our country with military bases and threatened us with nuclear weapons. Now they were to learn what it feels like to have enemy missiles pointed at oneself. We did not want anything more or less than for them to have a taste of their own medicine."[13]

At the same time, Khushchev was also very interested in arms restrictions and disarmament. In his eyes they were urgent "in order to reduce the pressure of

military expenditures on our economy and finally help the Soviet people to a better life."[14] He was sure that his own performances would be judged by whether
and how well he succeeded. Ever since the detonation of the first Soviet hydro-
gen bomb in September 1953, he was worried about a nuclear catastrophe, and
he concluded that an arrangement with the West had to be found by all means:
"Either peaceful co-existence or the most destructive war in history—there is no
third way."[15] He based his offensives on the conviction that a durable arrangement was possible after the confrontation with the Western powers. After the
confrontation had been managed, he was indeed able to find a common terminology with Eisenhower in Camp David and later with Kennedy after the settlement of the missile crisis.[16]

*Armament Dynamics and Economic Development*

Under Leonid Brezhnev the Soviet interest in arms restrictions did not appear so
clear cut. A Soviet military-industrial complex developed its own momentum,
which was neither slowed down nor directed by any political leadership. In comparison, the interest in economic cooperation with the West appeared ever more
prominent. Progress in détente became a gauge for the power granted to the general secretary. Urged by KGB-boss Yuri Andropov, Brezhnev in the spring of
1969 turned to a form of détente which consciously included the Western Europeans and the Germans. "We have to build our house in Europe", Andropov argued as early as February 1968, "and that is impossible without Germany."
However, the European interests were not to be put against those of the Americans, as Soviet diplomacy so often had attempted without success, and the victo-
rious powers were not to impose a diktat on the West Germans. Rather, "thor-
oughly honest, trusting and dynamic relations" were to be developed, which
would also help the Soviet leadership in the "civilization" of its country.[17]

When in 1979 the intervention in Afghanistan was up for decision, it was not
only the appropriate recognition of the endeavor's hopelessness, on which some
in the Soviet leadership agreed, but also the concern about the breakdown of détente. In March 1979, Gromyko explained to the Politburo of the CPSU that the
military intervention in Afghanistan "would throw everything over board that we
have done in the past years in terms of efforts regarding détente, arms reductions,
and the like."[18] It was primarily because of the rivalries in the struggle for
Brezhnev's succession that it took place after all. At the end of October, Minister
of Defense Dimitri Ustinov began to argue in favor of a forceful intervention in the
Afghan civil war, which to him promised to be a quick success and at the same
time was to pave his way to the top of the Soviet regime. Andropov did not want to

quietly stand by, so he, too, began to argue in favor of the intervention. On December 8, the rivals were able to convince Brezhnev of the necessity of this operation.[19]

In 1981, it was the fear of the breakdown of détente that played in favor of the perfidiously skilful decision to leave the suppression of Solidarnosc up to the Polish government and Party leader General Woyciech Jaruzelski. As late as December 10th, Suslov, Andropov and Gromyko stated in the Politburo that "the sending of troops [could] not at all be considered." Andropov added: "We have to adhere to our position until the end. I do not know how things will turn out in Poland, but even if Poland falls to the control of Solidarnosc, that is the way it is going to be. [...] Primarily we have to care for our country and the strengthening of the Soviet Union. That is our main line."[20] The solidarity of the rulers and troops of the Warsaw pact, which had allowed for the intervention in the 'Prague Spring' of 1968, did not any longer work in view of the temptations of Western détente. It was Jaruzelski's own decision to suppress the democratization movement with the help of Polish troops—otherwise he obviously feared to be held accountable for the failure of "Socialism" in Poland.[21]

This already implies that despite their heaviness and the careless opportunist exploitation of liberation movements the Brezhnev years did indeed show certain learning processes. Gorbachev came to power as a protégé of Andropov, that is as the protégé of a politician who, as we now know, had played an important role in Brezhnev's background for years. His actions can only be understood as the acceleration of these learning processes which then led to a qualitative leap. *Perestrojka* followed *Uskoreniie* ("acceleration"), albeit not in the economic and social development Gorbachev proposed, but in the trains of thought.[22]

A "qualitative leap" means that Gorbachev learned to liberate himself from misleading ideological assumptions and exaggerated fears. He approached reform with constant learning from Western think tanks. When Egon Bahr for the first time met the recently appointed General Secretary in April 1985, he discovered that Gorbachev had already adopted Bahr's concept of "Common Security" which he had learned from Georgi Arbatov: "What he stated was astounding. A new way of thinking was necessary: superiority, nuclear as well as conventional, had become senseless, deterrence dangerous; the East and the West would only be able to find security together and then also to disarm. In short: much to my surprise, Gorbachev developed the concept of Common Security. It was his foreign policy concept, ready to be carried through."[23] Indeed, due to Gorbachev's efforts, far reaching détente in the international situation preceded the disintegration of the Soviet Empire.

*Missed Opportunities and Overcoming the Cold War*

Ambivalences and possibilities for change, of course, indicate that the West had a great influence on the actual course of East-West relations. And they generally underline the meaning of personal decisions, not only of both sides, but also of the allies and the respective opposition forces, as each played independent roles.[24] For example, the reconstruction of the negotiations on the creation of a Western alliance, of the reactions to the Stalin Note and of Churchill's peace initiative of the spring of 1953 brings out a much greater degree of openness of Western politicians for alternatives than has been previously shown. The importance of Konrad Adenauer and the West Germans for pushing through the notion of East-West bloc-building has become very clearly visible. Similarly, it has become clear that the building of the blocs also guaranteed the containment of the Germans, while a lack of trust in the suitability of this path as a means for solving the German Question has played in favor of the search for alternatives to the Cold War.[25]

The Cold War is full of examples of statesman-like ability, leadership, responsible acting—and for each of its opposites. Examining the respective mixtures of these traits with several of the actors, both in the East and the West, is extremely worthwhile. Ronald Reagan, for example, was able to cooperate with Mikhail Gorbachev—after he managed to deal with his fears and restored self-confidence of a society that had been traumatized by the defeat in Vietnam and the hostage crisis in Tehran. This was the essential effect of his arms policies, not the restoration of sufficient defense about which there had never been a question.[26] Reagan's development, therefore, shows an extreme example of the function of military armament in the East-West conflict: it was necessary for the reassurance of a basically uncertain situation and in order not to give the opponent any occasion to preventively obtain security advantages or to exert military pressure in order to push their notions of order. However, the degree of armament effort that was suggested by some exaggerated the level of threat perception by a mechanical notion of balance, and by the logic of the arms race itself. Fear was a poor advisor that often prevented the actors from recognizing possibilities to communicate. Misperception played a major role in the conflict's escalations.

Regarding the end of the Cold War it, therefore, has to be concluded that the West had undermined the Soviet system from above as well as from its Western periphery—albeit not in the sense of clumsy conspiracy theories or covert operations, but idealistically. Insofar as a victory of the West in the competition of models of order can be registered, for the other side it was self-liberation, which has may fathers: Western think-tanks and pioneers, Soviet reformers and activists of the democratization movement in the countries of the Soviet sphere of power as well as Western partners, who supported the peaceful discharge of the Soviet system. It is both misleading and foolish to disqualify the self-liberation of the people of the Eastern bloc as the defeat of the eastern side in the sense of the "Cold War" metaphor.

1. For general observations on the "New Cold War history" see my epilogue in the new edition of Wilfried Loth, *Die Teilung der Welt. Geschichte des Kalten Krieges 1941-1955*, Munich 2000, pp. 352-89, as well as Wilfried Loth, *Overcoming the Cold War. A History of Détente, 1950-1991*, New York: Houndsmills, 2002. For an excellent research overview in German see Jost Düffler, *Europa im Ost-West Konflikt 1945-1990*, Munich 2004. Stimulating interpretations from slightly different points of view can be found in John L. Gaddis, *The Cold War. A New History*, New York/London 2005; and Bernd Stöver, *Der Kalte Krieg. Geschichte eines radikalen Zeitalters 1947-1991*, Munich 2007.

2. On the oftentimes laborious progress in the study of the sources see in particular the information published in *Cold War International History Project Bulletin*, Washington D.C. 1992ff., also available under http.wilsoncenter.org. A wealth of information can also be found in Wojtech Mastny, *The Cold War and Soviet Insecurity. The Stalin Years*, NewYork/Oxford 1996; Vladislav Zubok/Konstantin Pleshakov, *Inside the Kremlin's Cold War: From Stalin to Khrushchev*, Cambridge, Mass., 1996; and Vladislav Zubok, *A Failed Empire. The Soviet Union in the Cold War from Stalin to Gorbachev*, Chapel Hill 2007.

3. An overview on new research can be found in John Lewis Gaddis, *We Now Know: Rethinking Cold War History*, Oxford/New York 1997; Georges-Henri Soutou, *La guerre des Cinquante Ans: Les relations Est-Ouest 1943-1990*, Paris 2001; Loth, *Teilung*, pp. 352-89; Loth, *Overcoming*

4. Investigated by Aleksei M. Filitov, "Problems of Post-War Construction in Soviet Foreign Policy Conceptions During World War II", in: *The Soviet Union and Europe in the Cold War, 1943-53*, edited by Francesca Gori and Silvio Pons, London/New York 1966, pp. 3-22; the whole text published in *Istochnik*, 4/1995, pp. 124-44.

5. Compare the article in: *The Establishment of Communist Regimes in Eastern Europe 1944-1959*, edited by Norman M. Naimark and Leonid Gibiansky, Boulder, Co., 1997; on the Soviet zone of occupation in Germany, Wilfried Loth, *Stalin's Unwanted Child. The Soviet Union, the German Question and the Founding of the GDR*, London/New York 1998; as well as Norman M. Naimark, *The Russians in Germany. A History of the Soviet Occupation Zone, 1945-1949*, Cambridge, Mass./London 1995.

6. Compare Galina P: Muraschko/Albina F. Noskowa/Tatiana W. Wolokitina, "Das Zentralkomitee der WKP(B) und das Ende der 'nationalen Weg zum Sozialismus' ", in: *Jahrbuch für Hisorisches Kommunismusforschung*, Berlin 1994, pp. 9-37.

7. Compare Loth, *Stalin's Unwanted Child*, pp. 79-84; The citation from the presentation of Georgii Malenkov at the founding conference of the Cominform in: *Das Ostpakt-System*, edited by Boris Meissner, Frankfurt/Main and Berlin 1955, pp 87-9.

8. Cited in Zubok/Pleshakov, *Inside*, p. 93.

9. For examples, see Loth, *Stalin's Unwanted Child*, passim, as well as, in the context of the coming about of the so-called "Stalin-Note", Wilfried Loth, "The Origins of Stalin's Note of 10 March 1952", in: *Cold War History*, Vol.4, No. 2 (January 2004), pp. 66-88. On the continuing controversy regarding this crucial point of Stalinist policies on Germany, Wilfried Loth, "Das Ende der Legende. Hermann Graml und die Stalin-Note. Eine Entgegnung", in *Vierteljahrshefte für Zeitgeschichte* 50, pp. 653-64; and Wilfried Loth, *Die Sowjetunion und die deutsche Frage. Studien zur sowjetischen Deutschlandpolitik von Stalin bis Chruschtchew*, Göttingen 2007.

10. John Lewis Gaddis only considers the second part as he infers unlimited ambitions and the inevitability of the Cold War from Stalin's profound distrust: Gaddis, *We Now Know*, pp. 25, 31, and 292. On Gaddis' return to a very 'traditional' point of view also see the criticism of Michael S. Sherry, "The Triumph of Democratic Capitalism without the Democracy and the Capitalism", in: *Reviews in American History* 25 (1997) pp. 531-6; and Anders Stephanson, "Rethinking Cold War History", in: *Review of International Studies* 24 (1998), pp. 119-24.

11. Minutes of the CK-official Vladimir N. Malin, presented by Mark Kramer on the occasion of the conference "Hungary and the World 1956. The New Archival Evidence", Budapest, October 1996.

12. Cited in Oleg Grinevskii, *Tauwetter. Entspannung, Krisen und neue Eiszeit*, Berlin 1996, pp. 23f. On the pressure Walther Ulbricht imposed on Khrushchev also see Hope M. Harrison, *Driving the Soviets up the Wall. Soviet-East German Relations 1953-1961*, Princeton NJ, 2003.

13. *Khrushchev Remembers*, Boston 1970, p. 494. Compare Aleksandr Fursenko/Timothy Naftali, *"One Hell of a Gamble": Khrushchev, Castro, and Kennedy*, London/New York, 1997; Loth, *Overcoming*, pp. 67-76.

14. Khrushchev in a conversation with his staff in the spring of 1959, cited in Grinevski, *Tauwetter*, p. 153.

15. Khrushchev at the 20th Party Convention in February 1956, *XX sezd'KPSS*, Vol. 1. Moscow 1956, p. 36.

16. Also see William Taubman, *Khrushchev: The Man and His Era* (New York: Norton, 2003).

17. Andropov in a conversation with the Germany-specialist Yyacheslav Kervokov on February 13th, 1968, whom he assigned the creation of a "direct line" to the

Bonn government. Cited in Vyatcheslaw Kervokov, *Der geheime Kanal. Moskau, der KGB und die Bonner Ostpolitik*, Berlin 1995, pp. 29f.

18. Minutes of the Politburo session of March 17th-18th, 1979, in: *CWIHP Bulletin*, No. 8/9, Winter 1996/97, pp. 136-45.

19. See Loth, *Overcoming*, pp. 157ff.

20. Exerpts from the minutes, in: *CWIHP Bulletin*, No. 5, Spring 1995, pp. 121, 134-7.

21. Also see Wilfried Loth, "Moscow, Prague, and Warsaw: Overcoming the Brezhnev Doctrine", in *Cold War History*, Vol. 1, No. 2 (January 2001), pp. 103-18.

22. Important for the development of Gorbachev's thinking are Archie Brown, *The Gorbachev Factor*, Oxford/New York 1997; Archie Brown, *Seven Years That Changed the World: Perestrojka in Perspective*, Oxford-New York 2007; Vladislav M. Zubok, "The Collapse of the Soviet Union. Leadership, Elites, and Legitimacy", in: *The Fall of Great Powers. Peace, Stability, and Legitimacy*, edited by Geir Ludenstad, Oslo/New York 1994, pp. 156-174; Vladislav Zubok, "Gorbachev and the End of the Cold War: Perspectives on History and Personality", in: *Cold War History*, Vol. 2, No. 2 (January 2002), pp. 61-100.

23. Egon Bahr, *Zu meiner Zeit*, Munich 1996; also see Wilfried Loth, "Mikhail Gorbachev, Willy Brandt, and European Security", in: *Jornal of European Integration History* 11 (2005), No. 1, pp. 45-59.

24. The specific meaning of European actors is emphasized in a conference project, which has already produced three conference volumes: *The Failure of Peace in Europe*, edited by Antonio Varsori and Elena Calandri, Houndsmills/New York 2002; *L'Europe de l'Est et de l'Ouest dans la Guerre froide, 1948-1953*, edited by Saki Dockrill, Robert Frank, Gerges-Henri Soutou, Antonio Varsori, Paris 2002; *Europe, the Cold War and Coexistence, 1953-1965*, edited by Wilfried Loth, London/Portland 2004; *The Making of Détente. Eastern and Western Europe in the Cold War, 1965-75*, London/New York 2008.

25. Also see Wilfried Loth, "Germany in the Cold War: Strategies and Decisions", in: *Reviewing the Cold War: Approaches, Interpretations, Theory*, edited by Odd Arne Westad, London/Portland 2000, pp. 242-57.

26. See Loth, *Overcoming*, pp. 165-72, 179-97.

*Odd Arne Westad*

# Ideas and Power: Soviet Inner Debates in the 1970s

This paper is a discussion of a small area of Soviet foreign policy: internal debates within the Soviet leadership in the 1970s. It will sound close to the interpretation given by Loth, yet both are significantly different from a conventional viewpoint. Indeed, the mainstream still enjoys much credit among many of our colleagues. According to conventional wisdom, the changes of interpretation that emerged from access to Soviet and East European sources—not to mention materials from the western communist parties—may afford us a significant degree of self-reflection. But, in my opinion, that does not apply only to the whole literature about the Cold War that was produced until before the 1990s. Namely, it may apply exclusively to books such as the one by Loth, *The Division of the World*,[1] So, as I hear that stimulating interpretations from slightly different points of view can be found in John Lewis Gaddis' *We Now Know*,[2] I believe that such differences are significantly understated. Indeed, we should emphasize that Gaddis' book is a quite different kind of text. It is a text which emphasizes how the Cold War was a moral battle of good versus evil, in which the good—i.e., the United States—finally triumphed for reasons that seem to me world-historically based; that is as just the way it had to be, as if it were the march of history that made possible the victory of the forces of good. And that, I think, is as far from Loth's analysis as it could possibly be.

But let us now come to the issue: that is, the 1970s. That decade is important for international historians because it is where most of the cutting edge research is at the moment. There are two reasons for that. There is the very prosaic reason that the 1970s is the last decade for which there is good access to source materials. The other reason is far more important, and it is that the 1970s appear to me as a period when we can begin to ask why the Cold War ended the way it did.

But the 1970s is also a period when we can begin to ask most questions about the structure of the world after the Cold War. There is a growing consent on viewing the 1970s as a global dividing line. Scholarship on that issue is mostly driven by agendas of political economy-oriented historians, like Charles Maier.

Certainly, at least, to political economists, some of the same questions do appear, and do appear very strongly, in terms of how the global economy is organized.

As a global dividing line, the 1970s started with the collapse of the Bretton Woods system in the late 1960s. A new system much more oriented towards the driving forces of the global international financial markets came into being. That system lasted until about a month ago, when flaws were suddenly revealed to a wide public through the collapse of Lehman Brothers and so on. The system was driven by futures, by derivatives—in its various forms—just the way it emerged from the 1970s in terms of the global political economy.

So there is more about the 1970s, since there is much research on those years, more than just the issue of access to new materials. There is also a concern about how the contemporary world structure emerges.

With this in mind, my question is very similar—again—to that of Loth. Why was it possible for the Soviet Union, over a brief period of time, to move from the extreme interventionism which it practiced in the middle of the 1970s—particularly in the Third World—to such a sustained and thoughtful critique of that approach in the late 1970s—starting with the war in Afghanistan?

That critique paved the way for the Gorbachev phenomenon. The people who came from within that critique of Soviet policy were the people who in a very direct way became Gorbachev's main foreign policy advisers, like Anatoly Chernayev and a number of other people. So how was this possible? And why has it never been possible for the United States to carry out a similar sustained and thoughtful debate about the interventionist urges that are built into American foreign policy?

The debate on the 1970s was wide ranging. Some of it deals with ideological elements on the American side: for example, the research by Frederick Lagevall and Andrew Preston about Nixon's foreign policy[3] and the tensions between Nixon's and Kissinger's slightly different versions of Realpolitik, and of the different approaches they followed while never deviating from the basic ideological elements of American foreign policy.

Détente was never intended by the Nixon administration as any break with Cold War policies of the past. It was just a temporary measure, that was undertaken in view of a perceived weakness at home—related to social unrest in the 1960s—and abroad—tied to the war in Vietnam. It was also a response to what was seen as a rise in Soviet power that could neither be changed nor modified. So if the US could bring the Soviet Union, on some issues, to agree on the limitation of competition, that would help the United States through a very difficult period. But that would not end the Cold War or end East-West rivalry and competition.

Of course, for those who listen to the domestic critique of détente, particularly in the crucial election year of 1976, as Jimmy Carter was elected President, it's very clear that the point of view of the American Right was that Nixon and Kissinger had given in on American values. Nixon and Kissinger were willing to negotiate with the Soviet Union up to the point where they accepted the Soviets as their equal. And this was not acceptable according to people like Ronald Reagan who ran for office for the first time in 1976, when he challenged the incumbent president from the Right.

Yet we must be careful not to take the right-wing critique of détente at face value, nor in terms of its results, and not even in terms of its intentions. One might criticize Richard Nixon correctly—and Kissinger even more so—for many things; but giving up the Cold War to the Soviet Union is not one of them. For Nixon and Kissinger, détente was a temporary measure, not a long-term strategy.

The other side of the American coin that we recognize now is the extent of the change in domestic views of America's role in the world during the latter half of the 1970s. On that, the literature has gone through a transformation. Well into the 1990s, historians still wrote about the "Vietnam Syndrome". It was assumed that the United States after Vietnam was in a very bad state in terms of foreign policy, and needed a temporary respite from engaging with the outside world—particularly the Third World. One article I remember from the 1980s talked about, "Interventionism Takes a Holiday". As the documents on the American side show, this was not the case.

That can be illustrated by a set of documents from summer 1975 where Henry Kissinger goes directly from debating the immediate consequences, in terms of refugees, of the fall of Saigon, to a meeting where he tries to set up an American or American-led intervention in Angola—actually, the South Africans were going to do the job while the CIA was to prepare the ground. There is absolutely no break, in terms of what was seen as the American policy—of the American view of what could be done.

Moreover, after the Reagan campaign of 1976, it was very difficult, for even those who had supported the basic elements of détente, to continue supporting or even using the term. When Gerald Ford ran for election in 1976, he banned the word "détente" altogether. That word could not be used. Some analysts have pointed out that, as the economy moved toward the market, the right wing had a much broader political strength than before.

Now, let us turn to the Soviet situation. As on the American side, in a slightly different context, there were two world views that made themselves felt from about 1975-1976 on. They have been given many labels. The terms "interventionist" and "non-interventionist" are too facile. Or, one might talk about a "positive" view of the world on the interventionist side—that is, about people who believed that the world was moving in the Soviet direction—on the one hand; and,

on the other hand, a "negative" or "skeptical" view of the world on the side of
the anti-interventionists. But even that is too simplistic.

What is very clear, is that the well-known series of seeming successes for
Soviet foreign policy—and particularly for Soviet Third World policy—in the
mid-1970s did not lead to the kind of interventionist policy that was described in
the literature before we actually got to the documents.

Sure, there were a lot of people who argued that the victories in Vietnam and
in Angola signified something, as well as the fact that all the former Portuguese
colonies—with the exception of East Timor which was invaded by Indone-
sia—were turning in the direction of the socialist system and showed a great deal
of reliance on the Soviet Union. And the Ethiopian revolution was soon added.
There were people—particularly within the international department of the Soviet communist party—who argued very strongly that what this meant was not so
much that the Soviet Union did not need détente. But, rather, the argument could
be made that this sense of global turn indicated that some of the processes that
Lenin had predicted two generations before were actually taking place. With the
sense of a deep crisis in the western capitalist economy, it is not difficult to understand that some people would be saying: yes, the world is turning in our direction; you just need to give us a little bit more time; you also need—(and this
is crucial to the argument of the interventionists, or positivists, or however we
choose to call them)—to protect international socialism from its opponents: that
is, from pressure by imperialist forces led by the United States, and from domestic opponents. So, détente is all right—the interventionist would argue: but just
as long as it provides a kind of framework where the Soviet Union may support
the global turn toward socialism, particularly in the Third World.

If you study events from the outside, these people did win the argument—at
least, for a while. When Soviet operations in Ethiopia started, in 1977, that was
the biggest Soviet involvement outside the Soviet bloc but that was also the biggest foreign aid operation that the Soviet Union had undertaken since its aid to
China in the 1950s. It was a massive operation: and, by the way, one that still
awaits its historian.

So, the Carter administration, and those Western European governments that
were concerned, were right to notice that the Soviets saw détente as no hindrance
from involving themselves in Third World countries. But here is where the archives come in, and what is found there is very useful.

As a matter of fact, even as that chain of Soviet successes was reaching a
peak—that is, since right after the battle of Quifangondo, where the Cuban and
the Angolan forces defeated the rebels and their South African supporters—we
see that there were people within the Party and within the Foreign Ministry who
argued that this was not so much a moment of opportunity for the Soviet Union

as a moment of danger. Interestingly enough, those people also belonged to the KGB and other intelligence services.

Their argument was threefold. First, and by far the most important one, was ideological: if this was the moment that Lenin had predicted, why are we looking at revolution in Ethiopia? We're not looking at a revolution in Germany; we are just looking at a trend towards the left in Mozambique, but we were not able to sustain victories for the left in Portugal.

These kinds of questions lead to a profound ideological argument. That argument then led to: yes, there may be revolutions, they may be taking the world over and in the right direction, which is good, but this is not necessarily good for the Soviet Union, because these are not the kind of revolutions that were mentioned by the Marxist theorists.

In 1978, after the Soviets had, in a very decisive way, helped the Ethiopians with their war against Somalia, and were still arming them against their internal enemies, including the Eritreans, the Politburo appointed Andrei Kirilenko—who was then being hailed as one of Brezhnev's possible successors—to Addis Ababa. And his report is one of the most scathing critiques I have ever read of the so-called "real" socialism in the Third World. He had spent a day or so in a discussion with Meghistu Haile Mariam and other leaders of the Ethiopian revolution, and he came away distinctly unimpressed. That report is fascinating, because it starts by saying that he, Kirilenko, had spent time discussing Ethiopia's future but not so much about the war as about socialism, and namely about what kind of socialism could be built in Ethiopia with those people. And, about this, he says: "I must say, comrades, what kind of Marxists have we found?". What are these people? They certainly do not have a class background that predisposes them for any kind of Marxist thinking. They mostly come out of the army—and his Marxist definition of most army officers is petty-bourgeois *dilettantes*. They do not understand anything—and this is crucial—about the Soviet experience itself. They do not understand how the Soviet Union had built socialism. They had a narrow view of the opportunities that the Soviets saw in the world, which was also a way of heightening their own importance. So, after a scathing critique, Kirilendo ends his memo by saying that Ethiopia is not suffering from capitalism; it is suffering from a lack of capitalism.

The second point—and this is 1978, and not the 1980s under Gorbachev—is about resources. The more you take in allies with a socialist orientation in poorer parts of the world, the more you spend. And the question is raised again and again from 1976/77 on whether the Soviet Union can afford all of this while at the same time it is becoming more and more difficult to build socialism at home.

Thirdly, of course there is argument about what matters more and what matters less in international affairs. That leads to the ideological argument. There was much more, in my view, of a technical side to it, which still needs to be understood. Détente had given the Soviets relevant gains in terms of trade, and technological imports. Any single member of the Politburo—perhaps with the exception of Dimitri Ustinov—was hoping that the Soviet Union would reduce its military expenditure. That was dependent on détente. If there was only a little chance that any involvement in far-away poor places could undermine the mechanisms of détente—and here I am quoting Kirilenko—then it would not be worth doing.

So there is a three-level critique of Soviet interventionism, out of which came much of the ideological and theoretical arsenal that Gorbachev made use of—as I stated earlier. So, the question remains: if there was such a significant anti-interventionist lobby, why did policy not change before 1986, or perhaps 1987? The big question is about why the intervention in Afghanistan at the end of 1979 happened at all. Let me deal with that argument first.

I have no doubt that the anti-interventionists in and around the Politburo were in ascendance before the Afghanistan decision was made. That decision came out of a collapse—an atrophy—of the decision-making system. It came out of a political leadership that was so weakened—even in physical terms—that it was very difficult to stand up to that group who, for various reasons, mostly opportunistic, thought there should be a "limited military intervention" in Afghanistan. Again and again, it is the basic interventionist fallacy that was at work, very similar to the one that the Americans encountered in Vietnam, or in Iraq: it's very easy to get in, but how to get out?

That was a question that Brezhnev himself—in a brief respite of good health, proximate to sanity—started to ask himself, only a couple of months after the intervention took place. These are almost pathetic statements to his advisers: "You told me that this was an operation that would last two months. Why are we still there? Why are our boys still dying in Afghanistan?" No one could come up with the real answer, but that kind of argument then sustained the discussions.

That is one reason. The other reason is, I think, what was seen as a general hardening of the American attitude regarding the Cold War. We have already spoken about what I saw were the sources for that coming from the United States rather than primarily from within the international system. The more the Soviets came under pressure from the United States and their other opponents, the easier it was to justify the hard-line interventionist strategy—by arguing that one had to look after one's own interest, as détente was already in trouble. Sure, by December 1979, most members of the Politburo had given up on détente in its early form, which had existed since the early 1970s. And yet they hoped to rescue some elements of détente, and, if they had understood what the Afghanistan intervention would lead to, how much ammunition it provided for the American right-wing, clearly that question would have been seen in a very different light.

So there are two aspects to be considered to explain the Afghanistan decision: the international system, and the Soviet decision-making system. The important thing is these arguments, these issues, survived the freeze of the early 1980s. And as soon as the political climate within the Soviet Union at the very top changed, a new young Party secretary, who had not been a key member of the Politburo during the 1970s, came in, and the people he turned to from the very beginning were people who though not always were in agreement among themselves, had been critical voices with regard to Soviet interventionism in the 1970s and the 1980s. Again, a great topic for study. Why were those people the first that Gorbachev turned to? I think the explanation is that he knew that he needed an alternative, and these people were the alternative.

Which leaves me with a final question: How was this possible? My preferred explanation has to do with the development of Soviet political theory. This is a much neglected subject. Yet, because of the way the debate was set up, it should be taken seriously. Kirilenko's memo is just one example of the constant reference both to the earlier Soviet experience and to the central concepts of international affairs, which were part of the Soviet political discourse from its very beginning. And it seems that even throughout the Stalin period the Soviet ideological view of the world or of what made the world work the way it did—i. e. the basic Marxism that was still left in the Soviet Union—contributed very significantly to making the critique of socialism in the Third World possible.

Their view of the world may not have been correct; in fact, it was extremely skewed. But it did permit, and perhaps even fueled, that kind of critical thinking with regard to power, the notion that it is not always the case that, if you win, you win in terms of long-term developments, both for yourself and for the countries you intervene in.

Maybe that is where we should be looking with changes on the American side as well. Of course, that does not mean referring to Marxism, but taking some of those values that the United States was founded on, and discussing what does it actually mean to lead American foreign policy in the world. It is not just built on power; it is also built on a certain concept of how the world works, and that concept could be helpful when this new American administration is starting to formulate its own way out of the interventionist adventures of the last decade.

1. Wilfried Loth, *Die Teilung der Welt.Geschichte des kalten Krieges 1941-1955*. München: Deutsche Taschenbuch Verlag (1980). English edition: *The Division of the World 1941-1955*. London: Routledge (1988).

2. John Lewis Gaddis, *We Now Know. Rethinking Cold War History*. Oxford/New York: Oxford University Press (1996). See here Ref. 1 in the previous chapter.

3. Frederik Logevall, Andrew Preston (eds.), *Nixon in the World: American Foreign Relations, 1969-1977*. Oxford/New York: Oxford University Press, 2008.

*Rodolfo Ragionieri*

# An Actor in Search of a Theory
# Explaining Gorbachev's Decision Making in 1989

It is well known that neither the so-called "Kremlinologists" (i.e. the initiated in-terpreters of the Soviet *arcana imperii*), nor historians of the Soviet Union, were able to forecast the abrupt end of the Cold War and the subsequent disintegra-tion of the Soviet Union as a project, as a state, and as the successor to the Rus-sian empire. Meanwhile, many different interpretations have been given as to the causes of this relatively sudden collapse. However, it is well known among specialists that there is no real consensus about a satisfactory explanation of these events. After more than twenty years, the scientific community has failed to reach a consensus. I will argue that theoretical pitfalls can be overcome only by taking an innovative stand.

We can state that the main factor precipitating the change in the international system between 1989 and 1991 was certainly the new Soviet foreign and dom-estic policy initiated by Mikhail S. Gorbachev. This statement is almost obvious, but the causes of these policies are still open to political and academic debate. Moreover, what is unusual is that the collapse of the empire was driven by the center. It was Russia, Ukraine and Belarus that unilaterally decided to declare the end, without even consulting Caucasian and Central Asian republics. This im-plies that internal issues regarding full control of the leadership—and, in the Russian case, a personal rivalry between the president of Russia and the pres-ident of the Federation—were more powerful issues than maintaining the ex-ternal power of the state.

In my contribution I shall go through some of the basic narratives concerning the end of the Cold War. As I will try to show, each of them highlights some im-portant aspect, yet, none provides a fully satisfactory account of the events. I will finally suggest that only a process of learning and cognitive change could lead to the actual outcome. Moreover, from the point of view of the theory of Inter-national Relations (IR), I shall argue that only an approach that makes possible understanding cognitive change, and the interaction between multiple levels, is a suitable means for making sense of the outcome.

*Realism and its Discontents*

The simplest narrative of the change and collapse in the Soviet Union belongs to the Realist school.[1] One of the main problems in this case is the precise definition of "Realism". This is a very broad school of thought, ranging from Carr's and Morgenthau's more traditional and lengthy classical texts to Waltz's and Mearsheimer's methodologically refined texts,[2] and to the more policy-analysis oriented Steven Walt.[3] I propose we can identify five basic points that characterize Realism, even though they are not always explicitly stated:

(a) History and politics can be the object of a systematic, rational investigation;

(b) States are the basic actors, and the object of study is the relation among them in terms of power;

(c) Relations among states have an anarchic nature—i.e., there is no legitimate and effective authority above the states. This fact divides political arenas into two mutually excluding fields: domestic and international politics;

(d) Power is the basic issue in international politics; that is understood in many different ways,[4] but any scholar that defines himself as "Realist" does not cast any doubt on its relevance. Power relationships are more important than psychological inclinations or ideological preferences.

(e) The political sphere is autonomous with respect to the ethical one, and there is separation, or at least tension, between the two.[5]

Many different Realist narratives have been developed. However, they share a common ground, that has become standard commonsense in the media and among wide sectors of public opinion: power ratios were the main reason of the changes brought about by Gorbachev and his group. More precisely, the decisive thrust is to be found in the challenge posed by the confrontational policies of the Reagan administration. After a period of American retreat and uncertainty, epitomized by the Carter administration—so goes the narrative—Reagan challenged Soviet aggressive policies. His rearmament policy and his aggressive propaganda and foreign policy put such a stress on the Soviet military, economic, political and ideological system, that Soviet leadership had to catch up with the American challenge. This provoked, in turn, attempts to reform, that eventually proved impossible.[6] I shall deal with three main issues: first, whether there is any direct causal relationship between US foreign policies and Soviet reform attempts; second, how can we interpret Soviet gradual redeployments; third, the decision taken in Autumn 1989 not to maintain the "outer empire" in Europe at the cost of a confrontation.

The first problem with the Realist narrative is that a certain amount of time is always needed for a cause-effect chain to bring about its consequences. From this standpoint, the Realist explanation seems to be time inconsistent. In the Realist perspective, the main cause of the new Soviet foreign and security policy was the new confrontational American attitude and the stress it caused on the Soviet system. However, it is difficult to find any real response to Reagan's policies, especially from the standpoint of the percentage of the Soviet military budget on the GDP. To be more precise, the Soviet military budget during the 1980s did not change at the beginning of the decade—and declined later.

Let us take the example of the Strategic Defense Initiative. Reagan put forth his idea of a space-based anti-missile defence on March 23, 1983. But the basic problem with the Soviet Union in the first half of the 1980s (with the exception of few months in 1982-3) was rather the absence of real leadership, and the incapability to give a proper response at all the levels needed—i. e. the propaganda and communication level, the technological level, the strategic level. The old Brezhnev, the ailing Andropov, the nonexistent Chernenko (a pure mask of a declining and rotten system of power) were not the type of leader you imagine taking a strong reactive position. Perhaps the only exception was the attempts of a cautious reform put forward by Andropov in his first year as party secretary general.

Soviet reaction to the SDI was more propaganda than real. However, it was curious enough that Soviet propaganda stressed both the dangers and the impossibility of the SDI.[7] When Soviet security was perceived to be really at stake, reactions were more direct. For example, Andropov reacted to the Western decision to actually deploy ground launched Cruise missiles and intermediate range ballistic missiles (IRBM, of the model Pershing 2) in Europe by announcing the deployment of new Soviet short- and intermediate-range weapons.

There is no evidence for the belief that Reagan's foreign and security policy caused a Soviet reaction that brought the collapse of the system. There was no increase in Soviet military spending during the 1980s, and the decline of the Soviet economy started well before the Reagan era. However, if we proceed with that explanatory scheme—its weaknesses notwithstanding—the only possible way is to do so with a risk/benefit analysis which requires believing that political and military operational weaknesses exaggerated the effect of the Reagan propaganda offensive. It would have been suicidal to risk a direct confrontation with the West in the last months of 1989. As we have seen, this view of world history has many flaws; specifically, it does not explain why the Soviet leadership renounced its control of Central Eastern Europe—and, thence, its superpower status.

From a Realist point of view, what seems to have been lethal for the Soviet Union is the imperial overstretch of the 1970s—namely, the construction of a large fleet, the military build up (both in conventional and nuclear forces), and the pursuit of global politics.[8] This factor can be considered as lacking as an important component of national power. For example, Morgenthau considers quality of government and quality of diplomacy as essential elements of national power.

The gradual redeployment of Soviet strategic interests in the course of Gorbachev's leadership is another factor that can be considered from the Realist perspective. From the start, Gorbachev sought to redefine the basic strategic interests of Soviet foreign policy. For example, he decided to withdraw gradually from theatres (Latin America, Africa, and even the Middle East) that both critics and supporters of Soviet foreign policies had always taken as areas of forward defense of Soviet national territory. The decision to withdraw from Afghanistan seemed to be Gorbachev's least difficult—albeit unavoidable—choice. Anyway, the most momentous decision taken by the final Soviet leader was the virtual surrender of the last defence line in East Central Europe. Gorbachev not only gave the green light to the Jaruzelski-Solidarnosc agreement that deprived the Polish Workers' Unified Party (PWUP) of its former total control of political power in Poland, but also accepted the subsequent fall of the Soviet system in all countries of the Warsaw Treaty Organization (WTO).

The retreat of a major power from areas that are not deemed as essential is considered—for example, by Gilpin[9]— as a normal redefinition of foreign policy objectives by a declining power that cannot sustain the costs of defending areas whose control is not held to be vital for the preservation of major-power status. This might be the case for all extra-European areas—including perhaps Afghanistan. But certainly it was not this way as far as WTO states were concerned. From a Realist perspective it is almost impossible to explain why the leadership of a major power renounced its international status, unless this was necessary—or perceived to be so—in order for that state to survive. To make the statement more clear: from a Realist perspective, Gorbachev chose not to intervene in WTO states because this intervention might unleash a series of events leading to the destruction of the Soviet Union, or to its humiliation in international relations. This can be argued, but it does not fit with our knowledge of Soviet decision making in the Gorbachev era.

Moreover, if we look at world history, it is almost impossible to find the case of any great power whose ruling elite would decide to withdraw from areas deemed vital to its security, rather than trying to play the aggressive strategy—i.e., solving an internal crisis by means of external aggression or violent reassessment of control over the "vital" area.

A sounder version of a Realist explanation can be given in the framework of classic or "neo-classic" Realism.[10] The unit of analysis is the State (the Soviet Union); the object of analysis is decision making; and the independent variable is the *perception* of power distribution and its variations. The decisive factors were the perception of economic decline and the overextension of strategic commitments in the 1970s. The perception of the costs needed to maintain the status quo was more than proportional to the perception of decline. At the beginning Gorbachev and the group around him did not intend to initiate a radical reform course. But a feedback process took place almost against their will: measures were taken that made the perception of decline even stronger, and this forced the group to opt for more radical policies. All this explains how the Soviet Union arrived at the turning point of 1989, but does not explain how and why the leadership made the choice to renounce its great power status. In my opinion, this explanation goes beyond the limits of Realism, because it takes into consideration perceptual and domestic variables that characterize other approaches in IR—pluralism, for example. Gorbachev had other options. For example, he could have supported reform or even a departure from the Soviet model, but on condition that the WTO be preserved. We can conclude that "the Realist contention that Gorbachev's domestic reform was an 'externally imposed necessity' is conceptually and empirically flawed. It is outside any Realist theory and is not logically derived from Realist assumptions".[11]

In any case, Gorbachev's grand strategy was different with respect to traditional Soviet options, as well as with respect to policies characterizing other declining powers. For example, the Byzantine empire never decided to give up or not to fight for such vital territories as those in Anatolia—territories that were lost after a chain of disastrous defeats against the Turks, starting from Manzikert in 1071 and ending more than a century later (1176) in Miriokefalon.

In conclusion, the ideological, technological-military and media offensive that characterized the Reagan administration until the Reykjavik summit in 1986 had emphasized the weaknesses of the Soviet system, and the impossibility to continue a policy of stagnation and bare survival. However, it did not make inevitable a reform in a cooperative direction. On the contrary, until Chernenko's death in 1985, this policy was one of the factors enabling strongly conservative options—at the ideological, domestic and "imperial" level—that were only partially balanced by a discourse on "peace and disarmament" that concealed only the interests of a declining power.

### Semi-Serious Reflections on Contrasting Cycles

A direct use of many different standard cycles theories[12] would have unmistakably indicated that no direct clash between two major powers for hegemony in world politics would take place at the end of the 20th century. Many doubts

can be cast upon a rough use of cycles in the European system within the contemporary global system: for example, duration in time should depend upon the
characteristics of the system, and the global system of the 1950s-1980s is fairly
different from the Europe-centred system between the end of the 15th century and
1945. Other theories[13] could have pointed to a Soviet propensity to take the military
initiative, since Soviet growth was dramatically slowing down.

There is, however, the 12 years-cycle puzzle. The first big crisis of the Soviet
system took place in 1956, with Khrushchev's denunciation of the Stalinist system
at the CPSU's 20th congress, protest in Poland and open revolution in Hungary.
The second main crisis took place in 1968, at the same time with general protest
in Western countries. As it is well known, the most dramatic events took place in
Czechoslovakia with the so called Prague spring and the subsequent Soviet intervention in August of the same year, supported and somewhat instigated by the e-
lites of five other WTO countries—especially Poland and the GDR. This makes
sense because crisis and protest had already taken place in Poland, with a harsh
anti-Semitic reaction guided by General Moczar. This second phase of crisis saw
its final moment with the strikes in Poland in 1970, the repression and Wladys-
law Gomulka's (secretary general of PWUP[14]) substitution with the moderately
reformist Edward Gierek. The next crisis was in Poland between the summer of
1980 and December 1981, when General Wojciech Jaruzelski, under Soviet
pressure, declared the emergency state. If one examines this progression in time
and space, the final point should be clear: the end of the Soviet Union in 1992!

If we consider that the Soviet Union was dissolved on December 26,1991, the
twelve years' cycle is to a large degree empirically confirmed. The problem with
this cycle is that it has no theoretical foundation. But it is the only possible tool
that allows us to give a quantitative explanation of the timing of crisis. It is a
datum in search of a theory, and proves the poverty of data without an interpretation: data without interpretation are much emptier than theories without supportive data.

*The Liberal-Rational Alternative*

There are basically three liberal stories about the end of the Cold War. The first
one describes the superiority of capitalism as a system over any type of planned
society or economy. A second type tells of the superiority of open societies versus
closed societies. A third tells us of reform and cooperation. Paradoxically, a
Marxist interpretation[15] stresses factors that are economical in character. Eric
Hobsbawm underlines the evident "contradiction between production forces and
production relations" that characterized Soviet society. In this connection the
British historian entangles himself a bit: the failure of Socialism is attributed to

its existence in only one country (that was at the same time a choice and a necessity) and to the conditions in Russia—which demanded socialism in more than one country.

Ralf Dahrendorf tells us the second story. The German-British scholar, among the noble fathers of European liberalism, gave his own account of the fall of Communism in Central Europe in a much-quoted short book, written as a letter to "a friend in Warsaw."[16] His point is that the fall of those regimes was inevitable not because of the superiority of capitalism as a system over other economical or social systems,[17] but because people opted for an open society. For Dahrendorf, the Soviet renunciation of its superpower role was not a theoretical question. Even though he acknowledges that peaceful change (with the exception of Romania) was possible because of Gorbachev's renunciation of the Brezhnev doctrine of "limited sovereignty", he clearly sees this as part of a general trend towards a liberal open society—which made inevitable the measures taken by Gorbachev, in historical perspective.

A third alternative analysis of Soviet decision making in Autumn 1989 decisively points to a rational and reasonable consideration of the perspectives of Soviet economy and of the global ratio of forces. The apparent Soviet inferiority with respect to the US in military and information technology would have forced the leadership to make the choice for a more cooperative approach. A consistently cooperative Soviet foreign policy could not be reversed by an adventurous and risky revival of power politics just when the new policy was put to its most serious test: facing political change in East Central Europe.

The story runs approximately this way: in the decades of American-Soviet arms race and arms control a whole class of negotiators developed, more prone to cooperative than to confrontational strategies. This class was only instrumental to some policies during the Brezhnev era, but managed to take control of Soviet foreign policy with Mikhail S. Gorbachev. Once in control, this group, represented at the international level by Gorbachev and Shevarnadze, could implement the policies it had developed during the long years of so called Brezhnevian stagnation.

This explanation can be related to several types of rational decision-making: theory of cooperation in an anarchical system, coalition theory at the domestic level, and again the theory of cooperation in an anarchical system (in the framework of so-called institutional neo-liberalism[18]). It is obvious that ideas do play a role in liberal explanations of international politics.[19] First, they serve as road maps: they logically exclude other interpretations of reality. Second, they affect strategic interaction, as they identify some focal points that define certain solutions (see below). Third, ideas embedded in institutions specify policies.

This hypothesis explains very well the transition from confrontational to cooperative approaches in the areas of nuclear and conventional arms control, and the retreat from an aggressive stance in regional conflict. However, in this respect we meet a series of problems. First of all, even though Gorbachev's sympathetic biographers[20] tend to stress his inclination to a reformist view since his earlier years, it is not at all clear that he had always been the type of reformer he became later. Moreover, this liberal-rational explanation takes for granted the existence of different opinions within the Soviet leadership.

At the domestic level this explanation assumes a shifting balance in favor of reformists (for reasons to be determined, but presumably because of generational change), or that the domestic economic situation deteriorated to such a condition that even moderate reformists allied with a more radical wing—or just a pragmatic one, as we shall see below. This shift would have changed the distribution of preferences. Rather than any convergence towards a clear-cut winner (as in the case of the median voter theorem), we had one of the following possibilities: first, a shift towards pragmatism of the median point,[21] second, the creation of two polarized coalitions. In the latter case, hardliners remained unmoved, whereas reformers were forced to take more resolute stances, widening the gap between the two wings.

At the international level, the whole thing is basically explained by the metaphor of the insurgence of a sustainable cooperation between adversaries.[22] Nevertheless, all this machinery does not explain why the Soviet leadership had to renounce a superpower role. Theoretical analysis of decision-making in autumn 1989 will make evident that assumptions on cognitive continuity in Soviet leadership bring us to paradoxical conclusions. For the sake of simplicity, I assume perfect rationality, limited rationality, or incremental decisions.

In the case of perfect rationality we can try to analyse the situation by means of game theory. Instead of usual 2x2 games,[23] I put forward here a 3-players game. The players are decision makers respectively in the Soviet Union, in a generic country in East Central Europe, and in the West. The players are named G (Gorbachev), LL (local leadership) and W (the West, that is supposed to have uniform interests and strategies in this case). Obviously, LL's objective is to stay in power, even at the cost of a violent confrontation, whereas W's interest is a possibly smooth transition towards democracy. G's objective is reform, maintaining the Soviet superpower status. As usual, game theory should not be taken as an exact representation of real decision processes, but rather as a way of investigating strategies and preferences.

All actors can choose between a cooperative and a confrontational strategy, that I define respectively C and R (the latter would mean reaction for the West, repression for LL, and support for repression for G). Obviously a more complex structure of the space of strategies could be more satisfactory, but this can be enough. According to a method used by Diesing and Snyder,[24] first I write a matrix describing the possible outcomes of the situation, then I outline a realistic structure of preferences and analyse the corresponding three-actors game. I denote the eight different outcomes with the letter $o$.

| The end of the Cold War: strategies and outcomes | | LL | | | |
| | | C | | R | |
| | | G | | | |
| | | C | R | C | R |
| W | C | $o_1$: Regime transition in East Central Europe, Western- Soviet cooperation | $o_2$: Direct Soviet Intervention, assessment of Soviet power, Western humiliation | $o_3$: Wide repression and unrest in East Central Europe. Without Soviet support, possible violent overthrow of regimes. Passive Western attitude | $o_4$: Regime and Soviet control reassessment, Western humiliation |
| | R | $o_5$: Soviet humiliation, regime collapse, Western triumph, possible immediate disintegration of the Soviet Union | $o_6$: Direct Soviet Intervention, assessment of Soviet power, risks of war | $o_7$: Wide repression and unrest in East Central Europe. Western confrontational strategy, possible violent collapse of regimes with a Soviet minor role | $o_8$: Full confrontation, end of detente, consolidation of the blocks |

Now comes what is usually the most delicate part of modelling with game theory: the determination of preferences of the various players. In this case the problem is particularly difficult, because it was not at all clear what course the Soviet action would take at that time. Even such experts as the German analyst and journalist Theo Sommer wondered whether Gorbachev would pursue his path of reform (domestically) and cooperation (internationally) should a crisis develop:

> Should he stumble, or fall—would the rational new approaches of his foreign policy survive? Would the Soviet Union then just fall into paralyzing stupidity again? Or would it reassess control of its inner and outer empire by force? Would it choose again confrontation against the West? Even Russia's future is not predictable.[25]

As far as LL is concerned, we can assume that its basic objective is staying in power: the best outcome is staying in power without confrontation, corresponding to the strategy profile (C,R,R): Soviet support is necessary to stay in power. The second best is (R,R,R), where staying in power is paid at the price of a confrontation with the West. As far as the Western actor is concerned, I assume that a democratic transition under control is the best preferred outcome, because it would not have been worthwhile to risk a confrontation to gain marginal advantages. The worst outcome is obviously provided by a strong confrontational attitude by both LL and G, with a substantial Western acceptance of the situation, i.e. the outcome $o_8$, corresponding to the strategy profile (C,R,R). The most difficult to evaluate is the structure of preferences of the Soviet leadership. We must take into consideration two different and contrasting interests: the push for reforms and the willingness to retain a great power status.

If we think that local leaderships were ready to risk everything in order to stay in power, and that for the Soviets it was important to maintain their superpower role notwithstanding their weaknesses, we should write the following preferences (where ≈ means *is equivalent to* and ℘ means *is preferred to*):

W: $o_1$ ℘ $o_5$ ℘ $o_7$ ℘ $o_3$ ℘ $o_2$ ℘ $o_6$ ℘ $o_8$ ℘ $o_4$;
G: $o_1$ ℘ $o_4$ ℘ $o_3$ ℘ $o_2$ ℘ $o_8$ ℘ $o_6$ ℘ $o_7$ ℘ $o_5$;
LL: $o_4$ ℘ $o_8$ ℘ $o_6$ ℘ $o_2$ ℘ $o_7$ ℘ $o_3$ ℘ $o_1$ ℘ $o_5$

We get the following game, with an unexpected equilibrium:

| Tentative End of Cold War Game | | LL | | | |
|---|---|---|---|---|---|
| | | C | | R | |
| | | G | | | |
| | | C | R | C | R |
| W | C | (8,8,2) | (4,5,5) | (5,6,3) | (1,7,8) |
| | R | (7,1,1) | (3,3,6) | (6,2,4) | (2,4,7)* |

Obviously there is something wrong in the preferences: I have exaggerated the inclination of the local leadership to go the way of confrontation in order to stay in power. This means that I can leave everything as it is and simply invert LL's relative preference between $o_3$ and $o_1$. So I get the following game:

| The End of Cold War Game | | LL | | | |
|---|---|---|---|---|---|
| | | C | | R | |
| | | G | | | |
| | | C | R | C | R |
| W | C | (8,8,3)* | (4,5,5) | (5,6,2) | (1,7,8) |
| | R | (7,1,1) | (3,3,6) | (6,2,4) | (2,4,7)* |

The result is puzzling: either full cooperation, or full confrontation. However, in this case we can use the concept of *focal-point effect*:[26] players focus on an equilibrium they think more likely to take place. As we saw, ideas help to identify focal points. In this case, for example, the different risks of the two equilibria and the fact that the first one favours the two more powerful players. In any case, there is no precise way to exclude a confrontational outcome. Moreover, the link between the two levels of decision making (domestic and international) remains theoretically unclear and basically undetermined.[27]

An incremental approach[28] is even less capable of giving us a proper and convincing explanation: in a game of the kind I have just put forward, if we put the appropriate preferences we can get the desired Nash equilibrium, and thus we get some insight on preferences. On the contrary, in the incremental case the very nature of the process makes almost impossible the whole re-evaluation of the preferences that characterized Gorbachev, unless we can prove that there never was a real re-evaluation. If we look at the conditions defining the incremental approach, we can see that some of them do not fit with the Soviet decision making in 1989:

(a) Selection of value goals and empirical analysis of the needed action are not distinct from one another but are closely intertwined. Since means and ends are not distinct, means-end analysis is often inappropriate or limited.

(b) The test of a "good" policy is typically that various analysts find themselves directly agreeing on a policy (without their agreeing that it is the most appropriate means to an agreed objective).

(c) Analysis is drastically limited: i) Important possible outcomes are neglected; ii) Important alternative potential policies are neglected; iii) Important affected values are neglected.

(d) A succession of comparisons greatly reduces or eliminates reliance on theory.[29]

For example, we can think that, to a certain extent, (a) was verified, whereas certainly (b, c) are not a good description of that situation. Incremental decision making, among other conditions, does not take into consideration the possibility to re-evaluate the basic cognitive framework of the decision-makers.

Generally speaking, liberalism encounters problems if confronted with the need to explain the interaction between cognitive change and shifting strategies.

*A Counterfactual Narrative*

The role of individuals and their personalities in historical events seems to gain importance in two ways. First, the failure of pure structural theories; second, the crucial role of the preferences of the Soviet elite in the outcome of the crisis of Autumn 1989. In order to better understand this role, we can make use of a method that has been total anathema to historians and social scientists for a long time, i.e. counterfactual history.[30] All of us were taught that "history is not made by means of *if* and *but*". However, in recent years, counterfactuals have sparked some interest as a particular method to deal with the problem of assessing the causes of historical events and the relevance of different factors. In this case, I intend to highlight the relevance of individuals to the final outcome of the Cold War.

More precisely, the question is: what was the role of Gorbachev's, Shevarnadze's, Reagan's and Shultz's personalities, and what were the relations between them, in the particular and non violent conclusion of the Cold War?[31] One can imagine scenarios where, all other conditions remaining the same, the individual person Gorbachev is substituted by other Soviet personalities that could have been leaders of the Soviet Union at the time. In this respect two types of hypothesis can be put forward:

(a) Andropov or Chernenko had not died: a leader of the old guard was in charge at the moment of large upheavals in East Central Europe;

(b) the politburo in May 1985 had made a different choice.

Another possibility is provided by a change in American leadership: either a democratic president or George H. W. Bush was in charge, instead of Ronald Reagan. However, we simply cannot change history with the stroke of a wand, but we must imagine a scenario that changes the historical situation at a certain moment in some credible way. As we have seen, the postponement of Andropov's or Chernenko's death is a plausible hypothesis, but it seems a bit *ad hoc*. So we can maintain—in accordance with historical reality—a generational break in 1985.

A small change could have altered the situation at the moment of Gorbachev's election to General Secretary of the CPSU: if the Defence Minister, Marshal Dimitry Fyodorovich Ustinov, had not died of a heart attack in December 1984, he could have participated in the momentous meeting of the Politburo where Gorbachev was elected. In that case, a coalition guided by such men as the already quoted Ustinov, the seemingly eternal Foreign Minister Andrei Andreyevich Gromyko, and the aged and inefficient Prime Minister Nikolai Alexandrovich Tikhonov, could have elected a candidate more reliable for them—like the secretary of the party in Moscow, Viktor Vasilyevich Grishin, a hardliner, or Gorbachev's future rival Egor Kuzmich Ligachev, whom we could define as a moderate reformer.

A hardliner in charge at the Kremlin would hardly have set in motion a process of reform at home and of new détente with the US and Western Europe. In this case the scenario would have been totally different: a slow retreat and retrenchment, and further decline and stagnation at home. A moderate reformer would probably have set in motion some similar process, but what would have been the reaction to the Chernobyl disaster? The beginning of *glasnost* or the usual Soviet castling in a defensive position? And similar or even more basic questions could be advanced with respect to reform in the countries of East Central Europe.

*Ideology, Cognition and Change*

In the previous discussion I have tried to argue that:
    - purely structural, especially Realist, explanations, fail to tell us the whole story;
    - more specifically, the Soviet renunciation to maintain a superpower role is not successfully explained;
    - both decision making analysis and the counterfactual narrative tell us that individuals have a role and that types of preferences have to be explained.

We cannot know whether Gorbachev had already developed his cognitive frame of reference in 1985; in this respect you can put forward three different hypotheses:[32]
    (a) Gorbachev had always been a convinced radical reformer;
    (b) He changed his view of international security issues during his career within the Soviet establishment;
    (c) He had no precise idea about international security when he came to power, although he was among the supporters of domestic reform.

The first hypothesis would suggest that during the years of "Brezhnevian stagnation" Gorbachev had practiced the shi'ai tactics labelled as *takiyya*, i.e. concealing your own beliefs in order to pursue your ultimate objectives. Both the second and the third hypotheses imply a cognitive change in the Soviet leader. If you look at Gorbachev's ideology as it is formulated in his various speeches, you can note an evolution from a kind of "traditional reform", expressed in Leninist parlance, to a substantial acceptance of a kind of Western social democracy.

The traditional reform is a typical attitude to be found in declining empires or political units. It is the attempt to give new impulse to a stagnating or declining political enterprise by means of a declared return to the initial principles, and their actual re-interpretation. In this respect, Machiavelli writes that republics have to come back to their original principles:

> There is nothing more true than that all the things of this world have a limit to their existence; but those only run the entire course ordained for them by Heaven that do not allow their body to become disorganized, but keep it unchanged in the manner ordained, or if they change it, so do it that it shall be for their advantage, and not to their injury. And as I speak here of mixed bodies, such as republics or religious sects, I say that those changes are beneficial that bring them back to their original principles. And those are the best-constituted bodies, and have the longest existence, which possess the intrinsic means of frequently renewing themselves, or such as obtain this renovation in consequence of some extrinsic accidents. And it is a truth clearer than light that, without such renovation, these bodies cannot continue to exist; and the means of renewing them is to bring them back to their original principles.[33]

This is a very acute analysis of the relationship between the renovation and survival of a republic. However, in this respect, Machiavelli was probably a bit optimistic with respect to the possibility for certain republics to get back "to their original principles". However, historical experience proves that traditional reform simply does not work because *si duo faciunt idem non est idem*. As stated above, a presumed revival of original principles always implies their re-interpretation and often idealization.

When the Ottoman Empire started to decline in the XVII century, the first idea was to bring it back to its original source of inspiration, i.e. Islam and original Ottoman military and economic organization. In that case, however, traditional reform was always associated with a stronger control of the imperial center over the periphery and the rest of society. This idea lasted for at least a century, until Ottoman ruling elites started to understand the superiority of Western organization: first from the military standpoint and, later (in the *Tanzimat* era) in the whole organization of the State.

In the Soviet Union the transition from "traditional reform" to the acceptance of Western values and organization of State and society took a much shorter time. For a certain period of time Gorbachev paid at least lip service to "Leninism".[34] This was evident in situations like the 27th congress of the party, at the beginning of his path as General Secretary of the CPSU. Still in his introduction to the book *Perestroika* he stressed that Lenin's thought was his main source of inspiration.[35] Gradually, he changed towards a Western-like democratic or social-democratic way of thinking. This change was by no means forced. Theoretically, he could have chosen a Chinese way—i.e. a radical economic reform under strong political control of the center. We have more than twenty years of historical experience that this kind of policy is not appreciated by the Western powers, but it is accepted as far as it guarantees economic and political stability.

As we have seen, this kind of change cannot be properly explained by traditional Realist or Liberal approaches. At this point the reader might think that we are facing an uncomfortable choice among three possibilities: an approximate patchwork of different theoretical points of view, a pure deconstruction of failed theories, and a pure descriptive approach.

To explain the overall change in Soviet foreign policy, we must take into account not only one, but all the levels of analysis: individual, state and system, and a theoretical approach within social sciences that makes possible cognitive change. This approach is certainly constructivism,[36] i.e. the idea that substantive and normative beliefs concerning the social world structure determine our social action and interaction. Thus, change does not depend only upon material condition or capabilities: "To a certain extent, the social construction of reality that assigns changes in collective meaning and purpose to physical objects is itself an important component of the process of change."[37] Constructivism and cognitive theories represent an important novelty in the landscape of the theory of change in IR. In this perspective, anarchical structures and distribution of capabilities play a lesser role with respect to the cognitive structures and identities of actors, who produce, reconstruct and change the international scene

From the point of view of the individual, the generational change seems to be a basic variable. Brezhnev's generation had grown up in Stalin's era during the traumatic formative years after Nazi Germany's surprise attack on the Soviet Union and the terrible experience of the Great Patriotic War. Their original domestic experience was that of a regime that was not only totalitarian, but also characterized by pervasive terror and an abnormal sense of fear and suspicion. The external part of this conspiracy psychology and the idea of the construction of socialism in one country pointed in the direction of isolation and suspicion against all external actors. This obviously implied the impossibility of cooperation and a hyper-Hobbesian view of international politics, disguised under

Leninist terminology.

On the contrary, Gorbachev was a representative of the generation of the so called "20th congress' children". They were born in the 1930s, so they had some memory of the war, but basically they grew up in post-Stalinist years. They were conscious of the necessity of the transformation of an inefficient system, and they had come of age with the years of de-Stalinization. Many of them had shared the push for reform that had characterized intellectual and technical social milieus during the second part of the Kruschev's years. However, even though they generally and perhaps generically perceived the necessity of wide-ranging reforms, they had no clear idea about how to proceed. We know from Gorbachev's biography and from many witnesses that he was inclined to try new paths. In this respect, the key variable could be the cognitive complexity that characterized his tackling of the problems. We can use this variable to make the comparison between Brezhnev's and Gorbachev's thinking on security. Certainly Leonid Brezhnev had a low, almost absent, inclination towards cognitive complexity and change.

This is well proven by a comparison between the speeches held by the two leaders, respectively, at the 24th (1971) and at the 27th (1986) Congress of the CPSU. With respect to nuclear weapons and disarmament, Brezhnev took into consideration only two arguments, the destruction of nuclear weapons and the impossibility of fighting and winning a nuclear war. In contrast, Gorbachev was the first leader to use the word "interdependence", more than one decade later with respect to the Western academic and political debate. Even though this was done with delay with respect to the US liberal way of thinking, he advocated the establishment of a global security system on different bases than pure collective security.

These considerations prove that Gorbachev was ready to change his cognitive framework, but probably modified his views gradually, according to our third hypothesis. The different attitude of the new generation and the strong determination to reform the system set in motion the process at the state level, causing also the establishment of new alliances and alignments. As we saw, this new group was also more inclined to a foreign policy of détente. At this point the determination to bring about effective reforms and foreign policies, together with an inclination to change one's attitude, could set in motion the process culminating in the decision not to use force in asserting Soviet dominance in East Central Europe.

*Epilogue: Post 1989, An Inevitable Collapse*

Gorbachev's grand and tragic (because unsuccessful) attempt to save what could be saved of the Soviet experience brought about the collapse of so called "real socialism", i.e. the post-totalitarian[38] system that was derived from the Stalinist system. Many explanations have been put forward for his failure: a majority are convinced that the system itself was not reformable (it is almost conventional wisdom), whereas others think that the reforms were initiated too late. Perhaps the processes that *perestroika* had contributed to initiate could be put under control. Perhaps such control would have come at such a price that it would be difficult to imagine. All types of social and cultural forces had been set in motion, like nationalism, social and political pluralism. The comparison with China does not work for many reasons. China did not have to deal with an outer empire, and its domestic change was not and is not related to foreign policy. In contrast, for Gorbachev it was impossible to make reforms at home, to have good relations with the US and Western Europe, and at the same time to keep under control the outer empire in Europe. The only possible conclusion is that the avalanche could not be stopped.

1. For a review, see for example William C. Wohlforth, "Realism and the End of the Cold War" *International Security*, Vol. 19, No. 3 (Winter, 1994-1995), pp. 91-129.

2. The reference here is to four milestones of IR from the 1930s to the 1990s: Edward H. Carr, *The Twenty Years' Crisis* (London: MacMillan, 1939); Hans J. Morgenthau, *Politics Among Nations. The Struggle for Power and Peace* (New York: Hans Knopf, 1948; 7th edition, revised by Kenneth W. Thompson and David Clinton: Boston: McGraw-Hill, 2006)); Kenneth N. Waltz, *Theory of International Politics* (Reading: Addison Wesley, 1999); John J. Mearsheimer, *The Tragedy of Great Power Politics* (New York: Norton, 2001).

3. See for example Stephen M. Walt, *Taming American Power: The Global Response to U.S. Primacy* (New York, Norton, 2005), or his blog in the web page of *Foreign Policy*, walt.foreignpolicy.com.

4. See for example the differences between Morgenthau and Waltz: Morgenthau has a more subtle, multidimensional idea of power, whereas Waltz tends to identify it with military capabilities.

5. This definition is perhaps simplistic. For a deeper critical insight in Realist thought, see for example Stefano Guzzini, *Realism in International Relations and International Political Economy: the Continuing Story of a Death Foretold* (London-New York, Routledge, 1998); Richard Ned Lebow, *The Tragic Vision of Politics : Ethics, Interests, and Orders* (Cambridge/New York: Cambridge University Press, 2003).

6. The reason why reform failed is often reputed outside the reach of IR. However, most scholars attribute this failure to the intrinsic inefficiency of the Soviet economic and political system.

7. Probably Soviet scientists thought it was possible for the United States to develop a partial defence against incoming ballistic missiles, making ineffective a Soviet retaliatory strike, and so weakening mutual deterrence, see Raymond L. Garthoff, *Détente and Confontation. American-Soviet Relations from Nixon to Reagan* (Washington DC: The Brookings Institution, 1985), pp. 1026-8. For a Soviet position see Roald Z. Sagdeev, Oleg F. Prilutzkii "Strategic Defense and Strategic Stability", *Scientia*, Vol. 120, V/XII !985, pp. 371-6.

8. Overstretch can be interpreted better in terms of Paul Kennedy's vision of great power evolution, see Paul Kennedy, *The Rise and Fall of the Great Powers : Economic Change and Military Conflict from 1500 to 2000* (New York: Vintage Books, 1987).

9. Robert Gilpin, *War and Change in World Politics* (Cambridge/New York: Cambridge University Press, 1981).

10. Wohlfort, *cit.*

11. Richard Ned Lebow, "The Long Peace, the End of the Cold War, and the Failure of Realism", *International Organization*, Vol. 48, No. 2 (Spring, 1994), pp. 249-77.

12. See Joshua S. Goldstein, *Long Cycles: Prosperity and War in the Modern Age* (New Haven: Yale University Press, 1988).

13. Charles Doran, *System in Crisis. New Imperatives of High Politics at Century's End*, (Cambridge/New York: Cambridge University Press, 1991).

14. Poland's Communist Party had been forcefully disbanded by Stalin in 1938. The leadership was previously totally eliminated because of alleged infiltration of spies and the party disbanded under the charge of "Trotskysm".

15. See for example Eric Hobsbawm, *Age of Extremes. The Short Twentieth Century* (New York: Pantheon Books, 1994).

16. Ralph Dahrendorf, *Reflections on the Revolution in Europe* (London: Chatto & Windus, 1990).

17.With respect to this point his polemic reference is Friedrich von Hayek.

18. I refer here to IR theorist like Oye, Keohane, Snidal, and the first part of Axelrod's work In the huge literature, see Robert Axelrod, *The Evolution of Cooperation* (New York: Basic Books, 1984), Kenneth A. Oye (ed.), *Cooperation under Anarchy* (Princeton, NJ: Princeton University Press, 1986.) Later research by Axelrod is to be situated in the area of complex systems and agent based models, that can bring to similar results, but has different theoretical bases.

19. See Judith Goldstein, Robert O. Keohane, "Ideas and Foreign Policy: An Analytical Framework", in Judith Goldstein, Robert O. Keohane (eds.), *Ideas and Foreign*

*Policy. Beliefs, Institutions and Political Change* (Ithaca/London: Cornell University Press, 1993), pp. 3-30.

20. See Zhores Medvedev, *Gorbachev* (Oxford: Basil Blackwell, 1986).

21. In this case the median voter theorem (the winner in two candidate elections is situated exactly in the middle of preferences of voters) is used metaphorically, because we are not dealing with single issue plurality elections, but we can think of single peaked decision makers (one issue, preferences centred around one choice). See Peter C. Ordeshook, *Game Theory and Political Theory* (Cambridge/New York: Cambridge University Press, 1986).

22. See Axelrod, *cit.*

23. See for example Vinod K. Agganval, Picrrc Allan, (1992), "Cold War Endgames", in: P. Allan, Goldmann (eds), *The End of the Cold War. Evaluating Theories of International Relations* (Boston: Dordrecht, 1992), pp. 24-54.

24. Paul Diesing, Glenn H, Snyder, *Conflict Among Nations: Bargaining Decision Making and System Structure in International Crises* (Princeton, NJ: Princeton University Press, 1977).

25. Theo Sommer, "Leben im Fünfeck der Mächte", in: *Die Zeit*, 26.05.1989.

26. See Thomas Schellig, *The Strategy of Conflict*; Roger B. Meyerson, *Game Theory. The Analysis of Conflict*, (Cambridge/New York: Cambridge University Press, 1991).

27. See for example Thomas Risse-Kappen, "Ideas Do not Float Freely: Transnational Coalitions, Domestic Structures, and the End of the Cold War", *International Organization*, Vol. 48, No. 2 (Spring 1994), pp. 185-214.

28. See Charles E. Lindblom, "The Science of 'Muddling Through'", *Public Administration Review*, Vol. 19, No. 2 (Spring, 1959), pp. 79-88.

29. Lindblom, *cit.*, p. 81.

30. See for example Richard Ned Lebow, *Forbidden Fruit. Counterfactuals and International Relations* (Princeton, NJ: Princeton University Press, 2010).

31. This counterfactual narrative draws largely on Ned Lebow, *cit*, pp. 101-33.

32. See Janice Gross Stein, "Political Learning by Doing: Gorbachev as Uncommitted Thinker and Motivated Learner", *International Organization*, 48, No. 2 (1994), pp. 155-83.

33. Niccolò Machiavelli, *Discourses on the First Ten Books of Titus Livius*, Book III, Chapter 1, translation by Christian E. Detmold, (Boston: J. R. Osgood and Company, 1882): The Online Library of Liberty (http://oll.libertyfund.org).

34. As Marx was never a "Marxist", Lenin was never a "Leninist". Both Leninism and Marxism-Leninism were Stalin's invention of a tradition to be used in the ideological and power struggle going on in the Soviet Union.

35. Mikhail Gorbachev, *Perestrojka. New Thinking for Our Country and the World* (New York: Harper & Row, 1987).

36 See for example Emmanuel Adler, "Seizing the Middle Ground. Constructivism in World Politics", *European Journal of International Relations*, vol. 3, n. 3 (September 1997), pp. 319-63; Alex Wendt, *Social Theory of International Politics* (Cambridge/New York: Cambridge University Press, 1999). The obvious seminal reference is Peter L. Berger, Thomas Luckmann, *The Social Construction of Reality: A Treatise on the Sociology of Knowledge* (New York: Anchor Books, 1966).

37 Adler, *cit.*, p. 642.

38. In post-totalitarian regimes there is a limited but not a responsible level of pluralism, especially in mature post-totalitarianism. But rarely is there political pluralism; the role of ideology is officially present but strongly weakened. The models of post-totalitarian authoritarian regime change developed by Stephan and Linz were introduced to analyze democratic transitions in post-communist Europe. See Juan J. Linz, Alfred Stepan, *Problems of Democratic Transition and Consolidation. Southern Europe, South America and Post-Communist Europe* (Baltimore: The Johns Hopkins University Press, 1996), pp. 42-51.

# Panel: On Revisions and Comparisons

*Antonio Varsori*
A POST-REVISIONIST—OR REVISIONIST—REVIVAL? TO WHAT USE?

Both the interventions I have just heard and the abstracts I have had the opportunity to read seem to me very important and give some stimulating contributions. Yet, at the same time, they are very different from each other, and they are concerned with different periods and different issues. Nevertheless, I will try to find some common themes. First of all, they share a basic attitude about revising the usual interpretation of the Cold War, namely, John L. Gaddis' image of the Cold War as a moral battle between the good guys and the bad guys with the final victory of the good guys as a result of Ronald Reagan's determination. About this, I agree with Wilfried Loth's approach—which, in my opinion, is not very different from Westad's. Namely, I agree on the need to reach a better understanding of the viewpoint of those who lost the Cold War.

At the same time, I would make a critical remark. That is, there may have been the risk of going "back to the past" into some kind of post-revisionist interpretation. I am referring, first, to Loth's paper. I was struck by some words he used, like "perceptions" and "misperceptions". These were keywords of the post-revisionist school during the 1980s, which affirmed that misperceptions about each other's intentions were crucial in the origins of the Cold War: that is—if I may state it somewhat like a joke—it is assumed that there were good guys in both fields, and, had these been able to understand each other, everything would have gone well.

What about this re-discovery of the post-revisionist school—if not of the revisionist one? I see much of it as an odd debate, particularly because—just as Loth has remarked—the Cold War is now something we can discuss as a story with an end we know—not as a process which is still going on, like European integration. So, why do we need to re-discover revisionist or post-revisionist interpretations of the Cold War nowadays?

There is one more characteristic which is shared by the papers I have just heard and by those I have had the opportunity to read: that is, strong attention is paid to the losing side, mainly to the Soviet Union. I have been struck by Westad's contribution. He examined the Soviet political debate and the decision-making process. He tried to find nuances in the Soviet positions, which is important, because it is different from other usual interpretations, where it is assumed that these did never substantially change since Lenin onwards, and that the ultimate goal was never much else than winning the "war" and imposing communism everywhere in the world.

That fresh approach relies on a wide range of Soviet sources. We know how archival records *are* important. Still, we should never forget *events*. Loth states that, according to the documents, Stalin was seeking cooperation with the West, that Khrushchev was very thoughtful about peace, and that Brezhnev wanted détente in the 1970s. Westad has shown us that there was a tough discussion about ideology and policies within the Soviet Communist Party leadership, and that documents show how they were aware that the Soviet Union needed capitalism in the 1970s. He has also shown that the decision to invade Afghanistan was very controversial.

Yet, we must remember that, in addition to discussions within the leadership, there were also events. This kind of approach somewhat reminds me of the debate about the origins of World War II—I mean Trevor-Roper and Taylor. When was the turning point? Was it 1939, or was it 1933? Was the decision to start a world war already taken as the Nazis seized power?

In other words, if we don't look at facts, we can either find something, or everything. I am not a supporter of John Lewis Gaddis, yet some of the interpretations in this symposium leave me a bit doubtful. Some of the conclusions about the Soviet Union are that the Soviet leaders were able to change their minds and to develop a new foreign policy, whereas the Americans were not able to do that. It is as if we are making a comparison between somebody who attempts suicide and fails and someone who succeeds, and we say: wow, he was good; he was able to commit suicide. So, the Soviet Union was able to rethink its foreign policy, to change it; and the Soviet Union collapsed.

I also have a somewhat more serious remark. That is, everyone here points out the importance of the 1970s, as the real turning point—not just about interpreting the Cold War, but also in a longer-term perspective—as we refer to the crisis of America's world role, to the world economic crisis, and so on. The political debates of the 1970s were very similar to those of a few years ago. Obviously, they are different. What I think is important is the fact that the 1970s witnessed the origin of some historical processes which eventually led to the end of the Cold War. Clearly, the Cold War should have finished in the 1970s but very few people understood that at the time. But something completely different was happening, and that is what we are now trying to understand. A new world appeared on the horizon in the 1970s. Perhaps the Cold War was the last aspect of the old world.

If we look at European integration, the 1970s was also a turning point. From the 1940s to the late 1960s, European integration was pro-American—France under De Gaulle had been just the exception. It was, to be sure, a conservative and liberal process, tied to the American economic system. But after the late 1960s—and, of course, during the 1970s—European integration became something different. It was a *dirigiste*, and perhaps social democratic, European integration process. Just think of the Copenhagen EC summit of 1973. That was when Europe first attempted to develop an autonomous social and political alternative. That also meant trying to change the relationship between Western European states and the United States. It did not mean moving against the United States, but it did mean embracing a more autonomous European view of the world.

*Liliana Saiu*
ON AFGHANISTAN AND ENDING THE COLD WAR—OR THE "BIG GAME" AGAIN

What I'd like to do is to go back to some events of the 1970s. Westad has pointed out that détente was simply another form of containment—that is, containment from a position of weakness. It is very useful to underscore how many different perceptions, beliefs, and persuasions made the Cold War last so long, and to recognize how many chances for peace were lost—on all sides.

Regarding the main events during the 1970s, I would mention Ostpolitik, which led to the Helsinki agreements of 1975, especially the "Basket Three" on human rights. The Soviet leaders soon realized that "Basket Three" was an unaffordable price to pay in exchange for security in Eastern Europe showing that their vision was more tied to the past—for instance, the fear of Germany—instead of the future.

On the economic side, the end of Bretton Woods was fundamental, of course. But there is one other seldom mentioned yet important element. Between the late 1960s and the early 1970s, the United States came to the end of its oil surplus capacity. The oil surplus capacity allowed the United States to overcome international crises, beginning with World War II. But, in Cold War times, the Iranian crisis of 1953 and the Suez crisis of 1956 showed that this was not possible. The end of the US oil surplus capacity had far-reaching effects in the Cold War, and beyond the Cold War: it meant making new friends, as well as strengthening old friendships. The potential and the consequences of this fact can only be compared with the loss of the US nuclear monopoly in 1949.

It is also necessary to make a more general observation. The Cold War we know, the one that we are talking about, is not the only Cold War in history. After the invasion of Afghanistan by the Soviet Union, President Carter gave a very strong warning during his State of the Union speech in January 1980: the United States would firmly oppose whoever might try to challenge its vital interest in the Middle East and South-West Asia. I would call your attention to a declaration by the British Foreign Secretary Lord Lansdowne in 1903. You will find exactly the same words that were used by President Carter nearly eighty years later. So there was yet another Cold War, also known as the "Big Game", between two superpowers—Britain and Russia—over vast lands in Asia that stretched towards India. The words were the same: whoever tried to establish any fortified points in the Persian Gulf, would have to face the British army.

So, President Carter was almost bringing the world "back to the future" of eighty years and two world wars ago. Let us try to think of what was at stake at the moment when President Carter gave that State of the Union speech. It was security, access to resources, access to markets. That is, the elements that are always present in the history of international relations. We would do well to think of that Cold War, of how it ended, and why.

*Raffaele D'Agata*
ON POST-REVISIONISM AND ITS RELATION TO THE TAYLOR DEBATE

I would like to discuss a little more about a fundamental question that was the object of Westad's paper. It is now ascertained that there was something like an anti-interventionist current in the Soviet Union, which was composed of very experienced, competent, and cultivated people. These people were in ascendance during the late 1970s inside the ranks of the Soviet ruling élite. Let me raise the question again: why did they not prevail until it was too late? And why, on the other hand, did the anti-interventionist thinking in the United States not prevail until, maybe, the election of Barack Obama?

Westad has emphasized the importance of the international framework. In *The Fall of Détente*, edited by Westad, it was shown how the Soviet promoters of a cooperative multilateralist approach to the Middle Eastern crises were systematically frustrated and humiliated by US policies during the 1970s.

On the Middle East, the arguments of the Soviet anti-interventionists could hardly face allegations at home that cooperative and "moderate" policies had not paid off. That was not just a by-product of Kissinger's Middle Eastern policy. Rather, it was a consciously pursued target. That is, Soviet responsibility about the Middle East was seen as dangerously likely to increase Moscow's audience and authority, so it should be thwarted anyway—no matter what it might actually produce. Within this framework, it would be difficult to exaggerate the importance of the harsh reversal of US policy after the agreement that had been reached between US Secretary of State Cyrus Vance and Soviet Foreign Minister Andrey Gromyko on October 1 1977 about solving the Arab-Israeli dispute—a reversal that took place literally overnight.

That is why there is a marked difference between the themes we are discussing here and the so-called "Taylor debate" about the origins of World War II. Sure, one might add a whole series of variously oriented historians, ranging from Klaus Hildebrand to Jürgen Wendt and Detlef Juncker, who also argued for the "moderate" side of Germany's foreign policy in the late 1930s: that is, there certainly was something like an anti-interventionist lobby, or even a peace lobby, inside the Third Reich as well—let us think of people like Hjalmar Schacht, for instance.

Yet, in my opinion, there is a fundamental difference between those two cases. The practical conveniences for cooperative international policies were far weaker within the structure of Nazi Germany's economic and political system than within the Soviet one. In Nazi Germany, it could be argued that an interventionist policy of confrontation—and, namely, military operations abroad—could overcome any obstacle. In other words, "moderate" Third Reich officials had no easy job while trying to argue that such policies might endanger the inner balance of the Nazi régime—at least, as far as the *Blitzkrieg* system was functioning. Alan S. Milward's studies on this subject are still quite illuminating. In contrast, the Soviet anti-interventionists might hardly be countered in the use of such an argument. The reasons why they did not prevail soon enough were more complex.

But all this was not just a matter of convenience. Rather, it was just the intimate contradictory meaning of the Soviet experience. In my view, as Gorbachev finally declared something like "We do not want to be a 'great power' anymore", he did little more than state a contradiction that was inscribed in the whole history of the Soviet system, of the Soviet state, and of Soviet ideology. He might also have said: "We've had enough of that burden, let us now finally breathe".

Perhaps a similar scheme might be applied to explain why the anti-interventionist current in the United States found it so difficult to assert itself before the election of Obama—and might still face some dire challenges. While they are very intelligent and cultivated people, they also would find it hard to demonstrate that foreign military interventions are a burden to the inner balance of the existing American economic and social system. Rather, international tensions, as associated with a somewhat induced "supply of security" on the part of the US with reference to a wide set of allies, may also be recognized as a way to ensure a constant flow of foreign capital into the US economy—a flow which actually became a vital factor of US wealth and power since the 1970s.

## MORE ON SOUTH-CENTRAL ASIA AND THE "BIG GAME"

*Gian Paolo Calchi Novati*—Regarding the Soviet decision to invade Afghanistan, the Soviets were sure in 1979 that the US was going to intervene in Iran. This could be seen as a reason for their own intervention in Afghanistan. An expected new expansion of the "British" (or "American") Empire toward the Persian Gulf may have suggested that control of Afghanistan, once more, was essential to the "Russian" one. So, the two buffer states in the Big Game—Persia and Afghanistan—were still in the balance. Perhaps "Russia" was doomed to fall into the American trap.

*Raffaele D'Agata*—Perhaps a story of covert Iranian-American deals in the 1980s, which is still being given too little space in most current reconstructions of the last phase of the Cold War, should be discussed. In other words, the Iran-contra operation, the curious episode of the Bible that Ronald Reagan had sent to Khomeini, and so on. By then, it seemed that fighting Iran—either by means of Saddam's Iraq or differently—was seen as ill-advised, as it should also be ensured that the Western front of interventions in the Afghan civil war—where the Iranians were also involved—would continue to be active.

# SECTION II

# WHAT STAKES DID THE "WINNERS" GAIN?

*Raffaele D'Agata*

# Ostpolitik, Euro-Communism, and Détente: Responding to the World Crisis

The great slump that engulfed the world economy during the early 1970s was the culmination of a disparate set of processes that had for nearly a century determined the fundamental issues of public debate and many features of everyday life in the developed countries. This slump shook and displaced basic elements of both capitalism and—accordingly, if unadmittedly—the half-century long Soviet communist attempt at suspending capitalist rules. The way capitalism survived the crisis of the 1930s and through World War II was its incorporation of elements of the socialist challenge in terms of public policies that promoted full employment and state supervision of market trends and activities. Words that describe the rapid pace of change could not keep up with the changes themselves. As a consequence people were just as misled then as historians may be today.

I will concentrate on how change has affected the actual meaning of the East-West conflict—that is, the basis upon which European politics has rested for at least a quarter century. So great was the change that such terms as "the West" or "Western civilization" simply ceased to mean anything concrete—if they ever had.

The most common meaning of those terms had been significantly modified soon after World War II, as the meaning was deeply influenced by the internationalist foreign policy of the Truman administration and its reception in Western Europe. By the end of the 1940s, a widespread consent appeared on both sides of the Atlantic qualifying as "western". It was the mix of individual rights and public concern about the less fortunate that evolved through the steady effectiveness of New Deal policies—and through their reception in Western Europe along with the Marshall Plan.

Previously neither "the West" nor "Western civilization" was seen as based on any prevailing liberal concepts. Rather, they seemed closely associated with a set of radically conservative views. Oswald Spengler's book on the subject was a case in point. Throughout the first half of the twentieth century, the ghost of so-called "mass" society was often related to some sort of un-western and namely

"Asian" threat. And, during the last stages of World War II, Nazi and Fascist leaders and proponents even went so far as depicting themselves as the champions of some sort of "European" and "western" final struggle against any Bolshevik and hence "Asian" attempts at domination. That might explain Franklin D. Roosevelt's constant omission of any "western" characterization of the kind of world civilization he was promoting through the Atlantic Charter, the Four Freedoms' Speech, and the United Nations.

The "western" characterization of the prevailingly liberal side of Trans-Atlantic consent during the late 1940s should not be viewed as anything so obvious. McCarthysm was not accidental. Nor were a lot of intellectual efforts aimed at amending the liberal tradition from compromise and moral doubt, while showing their ability to learn from some form of religious integrity. Of these religious influences, the most militant, like political Islam, were soon appreciated, by key influencial US civil and military officials.[1]

These elements were significant while those features of the Atlantic consent that have been mentioned above as typically liberal were melted into a complex pattern referred to as the so-called "liberal empire". Of course, "liberal empire" is an oxymoron—which is by no means any exception whenever historical complexities must be named. Flaws soon appeared which could undermine the typically liberal approach. That is, the "western" Cold War empire finally turned out to be not liberal enough to keep it away from a kind of entangling intimacy somewhere between the realm of power and the realm of belief. Such flaws were somewhat underestimated during the earliest phase of American leadership within the Atlantic community—owing to the steady momentum of the New Deal coalition in American politics and culture, and the multiple transatlantic feedback that made the momentum effective on a world scale for nearly 20 years since the end of World War II. The Great Slump of the early 1970s was a fatal blow to that confidence as well. A period of unrest began, until power and belief were found to be strikingly merged together during the early 2000s, to an extent that certainly did not meet liberal standards.

Thus, pious atheists and power-greedy believers finally advanced shoulder-to-shoulder to call for ill-defined wars in some god's name just after a quarter-century-long period of turbulent reshaping of the world economic and political system. That fuzzy partnership had been growing along with a lot of reckless gambling in the economic field. Yet, such an end was and is no end at all. Many different paths were explored in the wake of the Great Slump until the Atlantic Community—and a lot more—were driven into the present conditions.

The Atlantic community was led through the earliest shocks of the Great Slump by Richard Nixon's and Henry Kissinger's perceptions about the requirements and the purposes of American influence on world affairs. According to

Kissinger's realist view, American power was actually driven away from any intimacy with the realm of belief. And so was the American supply of leadership within the Atlantic community—along with the American interpretation of any "western" common meaning.

For those with liberal expectations, this was a mixed blessing. On the one hand, a number of cold-war constraints, reasons for anxiety, were somewhat lifted—through arms control negotiations and some steps toward softening East-West tensions. Yet, on the other hand, new constraints were created that limited the range of viable options on how to face the world crisis, and the related need for sweeping changes.

As stakes were now being put in terms of crude national and corporate interests,[2] both loyalties and hostilities might become more binding and more demanding than if measured in terms of ideological or moral requirements. The former, of course, might be far less reactive to any intellectual challenge. Under the Nixon administration, US policies were more suspicious of Western European left-wing political tendencies than under Truman's and Eisenhower's administrations—not to say Kennedy's and Johnson's. In fact, European left-wing parties were either softening their opposition to NATO or actually supporting government policies which included NATO commitments. The latter was the case of the German socialists (who had been firmly opposing NATO during the 1950s), while the Italian communists were following approximately the same path at an increasing pace—only to be vetoed out of any power-sharing with increased determination from Washington.

Specifically, a US ban against any communist power-sharing in Italy was implemented by all means, including covert action, regardless of whatever Italian Communist Party leaders might declare or demonstrate through actual behavior regarding commitments to western-style democracy. As it turned out, such issues became much less significant than they were before.

A wholesome left-wing orientation within European politics was manifested through such developments as the German social democrats' access to power in 1969 and the increasing credibility of the Italian Communist Party as a factor of democratic change in their country. It was no accident that the Italian Communist Party was increasing its influence alongside an engaging dialogue with the German social democrats—which also exacerbated East German leaders. The Italian communists publicly sided with the attempt at democratic reforms in Czechoslovakia in 1968—which brought them to publicly disapprove of repression through the invasion of that country by Warsaw Pact forces. More important, they basically rejected whatever ideological argument might be made to justify the invasion, even though they might keep on talking with the Soviets about such shared concerns as stability and peace in Europe. The German social democratic leaders expected them to do just that—as they themselves were maintaining normal relations with the Soviets after the Czech crisis.

The Nixon Administration was upset by such changes. Nixon and Kissinger initially decided to swallow the initiatives of the social democratic leadership in Bonn to establish a shared ground of principles for peaceful relations with the Eastern bloc in Europe. Opposing these initiatives would hamper their own way of seeking compromises with Moscow as a temporary respite while the Cold War was being waged in what they saw as an unfavorable situation for the United States. At the same time, just as German social democratic leaders appeared to take the Atlantic consent too literally as a peace device, some western European communists might have become a problem in terms of their zealous advocacy of "western" ideas.

Actually, the German social democrats were practically taking the lead in setting the basic assumptions and the agenda for a new shared attitude among western European labor-based political parties since the late 1960s, especially regarding international politics. Using NATO as a device to ensure stability while pursuing change was a cornerstone of Willy Brandt's and Egon Bahr's grand design about overcoming the Cold War (as opposed to any victory in the Cold War). So was the pursuit of German national unity as a long-term goal through patient negotiation. In their words, Germany's role was one and the same with Europe's. The earlier "bridge theory" (*Brückentheorie*)—which had motivated the neutralist opposition to NATO in Western Germany—was now included within the framework of a newly interpreted and somewhat redefined Atlantic tie and extended to Europe as a whole. In Bahr's words, "Europe's weight would grow just as much as the importance of security problems would decrease."[3] Emphasizing the Atlantic commitment was consistent with that, as it might appease any understandable if unexpressed American fear that the German *Ostpolitik* might end up in some kind of self-sufficient and less market-oriented Eurasia. Accordingly, the whole system of the Eastern Treaties—as based on the principles that had been set down through the "Bahr Document" as early as May 1970[4]—involved the expectation that Moscow would not oppose some gradual changes affecting its relations to West Germany—if that would bring any economic returns as well as any credible warrants about the stability of territorial boundaries and of the military balance.

Ambassador Falin's attitude in Bonn was among the most encouraging signs that such a road might be viable,[5] whereas the most ominous indications usually came from other Eastern European governments.[6] On occasions, Brezhnev himself was moved to downgrade the significance of some Warsaw Pact official statements while speaking to West German negotiators. Thus, as Bahr reported on talks he had in Moscow by the end of July 1973, he thought he might use this chance to comment on the junior European allies of the Soviet Union: "They are not smarter than our allies: they fear to be sold off."[7]

While Brandt's and Bahr's caution was successful in fulfilling the institutional framework for European détente through the *Ostverträge* or "Eastern Treaties"—by exploiting American parallel interest at stabilizing the East-West conflict short of any further danger of uncontrollable crises—it never changed Kissinger's basic hostility to their policies.[8] That emerged at full light as soon as the *Ostverträge* were signed, and the unsolved Middle Eastern question was testing the depth and the scope of the wholesome détente process. Just as the Middle Eastern policy of the Nixon administration implied a strict delimitation of how global détente should be interpreted, it also implied a firm commitment to keep full control of how it should be treated and carried out by European allied countries.

The Nixon administration made it clear that they saw détente in the Middle East as little more than the way the bipolar conflict could be waged under the current circumstances. Whereas the State Department made some steps toward a more cooperative approach inside the United Nations during Nixon's first term, National Security Adviser Henry A. Kissinger successfully maneuvered to reduce them to mere window-dressing and to develop a quite different policy even before he directly took responsibility as Secretary of State in 1973. That policy was based on the assumption that Soviet cooperation offers and moderate behavior about the Middle East represented a threat rather than an opportunity, as they would make it hard to justify US pretensions to contain Moscow's influence in the region.[9] "We wanted to escape something that would have trapped us into agreeing", Kissinger explained to a suspicious Israeli ambassador just after Brezhnev's visit to San Clemente—where the Soviet top leader had unsuccessfully tried to persuade the Americans into some joint action in order to prevent an impending new war in the Middle East. That result had been reached —he added—through maneuvers he "wouldn't describe."[10]

Not all American initiatives before the Yom Kippur War might be comfortably described just for the Israelis: namely, no Israeli should have listened to what Kissinger confided to National Security Advisor Brent Scowcroft and Defense Secretary James R. Schlesinger just a few weeks before the Egyptian offensive. He sympathetically compared Anwar Sadat's problem with Israel to the one he felt to be his own while he was dealing with North Vietnam: that is, previously doing the enemy as much harm as was needed in order to reach something short of "unconditional surrender."[11]

Actually, the Nixon administration had been quick to evaluate the opportunity of earning Egypt's friendship. This was offered by Moscow's attempts at keeping Sadat in short supply of Soviet weapons to remove the option of a mil-

itary solution. This was compensation enough for the heavy amount of calcu-
lated risks to be taken by Israel while the Yom Kippur War was approaching.

Ignoring Brezhnev's solicitations for a joint Soviet-American peace-keeping effort might have appeased the Israelis given their refusal to consider a total retreat to the borders of 1967. But its main rationale was another: taking
maximum profit from the increasing difficulties that the Soviets were facing in
Cairo—and even in Damascus—because of their moderation. The main purpose had been to "frustrate the Arabs as long as they relied on Soviet arms and
pressures."[12] Accordingly, any possible Arab will to rely upon Soviet moderate
diplomacy should be frustrated even more radically. "Many say the Soviet Union has violated détente in the Middle East. The opposite is true", Kissinger
later said during a Cabinet meeting, as "the Arabs complain the Soviets didn't
do enough and therefore the Soviets are losing their position. Sadat", Kissinger
finally admitted, "threw the Soviet Union out in 1972 because he feared they
would keep him from going to war."[13] Indeed, as Kissinger later described the
Yom Kippur War as "unexpected" (not accidentally, during one of his earliest
talks with President Ford), he was making a very keen point.

For his part, Nixon had been less subtle. As he was back from a triumphal
trip in the Middle East—which might have somewhat compensated his Watergate frustrations—he told the Cabinet little less than the truth about the Yom
Kippur War: "Without our conduct in the October war", he said, "profound
change in the Middle East could not have taken place." And he also specified
that the war itself had been a convenient prerequisite to reach that, as it had
"demonstrated to the Arabs that the war couldn't do it and to the Israelis that
it was an increasingly unpalatable alternative."[14]

In sum, just as the Middle Eastern conflict was emerging as the pivotal issue that would influence world politics for years to come, the Nixon administration was treating it according to a priority list where the actual life chances
of the inhabitants of the area, and their relation to whatever concept of democracy they might have had, did not rank very high. In considering this point, the
pressing appeals for loyalty made to the NATO allies during the Yom Kippur
War and immediately afterwards might barely be related to any ideological assumption—and least of all to whatever extension of the idea of "West" which
had been the original ground of the Atlantic consent. As a consequence,
Brandt's and Bahr's neo-Atlanticism, which was a consistent development of
that early vision (and, besides, might be seen as a model for Italian communist
increasing openness toward accepting NATO), was bound to be totally ineffective—if not backfiring—as a way to appease American suspicions.

As a matter of fact, before the Yom Kippur War the Nixon administration
had been bitterly unhappy as Brandt was increasingly appearing to be willing to

contribute to make détente irreversible through its extension to a broader set of issues, including the most sensitive ones on a global scale. To Brandt, that also meant bringing the FRG to play an active role in order to favor a negotiated settlement of the Arab-Israeli dispute in the first place: namely, in order to encourage both superpowers to join their efforts toward implementing just the UN resolutions to which they had subscribed—and, meanwhile, toward preventing the conflicting parties from resorting to force once again.

That was not precisely a Nixon administration priority. As a matter of fact, Brandt's activities were also at issue during the confidential meeting between Kissinger and the Israeli ambassador Simcha Dinitz, soon after Brezhnev's visit to the United States. Although Kissinger was clearly in no position to tell the Israelis everything he had in mind by then—namely, the kind of dangers to which Israel was being exposed while he was striving to earn Egypt's gratefulness in the future[15]—both men agreed that Brandt was a problem, and that some influence should be exerted in order to see to it that things in Bonn might change.[16]

As trans-Atlantic relations became very strained during and soon after the Yom Kippur war, so did relations between senior government and SPD politicians in Bonn. In the few months that followed that pivotal earthquake in world politics, a fundamental showdown was played out both among western countries and among political visions and leaders inside Western Europe.

Originally, the German presidency of the EC Council—just since January 1st 1974—was expectedly reflecting the latter's orientation to promote the indivisibility of détente, and, namely, some extension of the Helsinki process to the Mediterranean—where the Middle East also belongs.[17] This was consistent with a widely shared attitude among European popular-rooted political parties. That was a cornerstone of the increasing understandings between the Christian democrats, the socialists, and the communists themselves, whenever key international problems were debated in the Italian Parliament in that period. This approach would have been called bipartisan elsewhere, and was among the motives for communist leader Enrico Berlinguer's proposal of an Italian Grand Coalition experience or *compromesso storico*.

Not accidentally, the German social democrats and the Italian communists had been multiplying their contacts—no less committedly than cautiously—since the beginning of Brandt's *Ostpolitik*. A sense of cautiousness was historically advised because of some deep-rooted ideological suspicions inside the West German Grand Coalition. After the early elections of September 1969, which permitted him to take office in Bonn as Chancellor, Brandt had hinted at intensifying those contacts and even at making them official.[18] Yet Brandt was too concentrated on reaching the goals of his Eastern détente policy—which also meant appeasing American suspicions—that he hindered the development of those projects. The terror blast in Milan on December 12, 1969, was also perceived as a sign of how deeply and how scrupulessly the basic political conformity of Western Europe might be preserved by means of parallel covert actions.[19]

In this, as Kissinger successfully pressed the Bonn government in order to obtain their alignment with his policies on the Middle East and the oil problems after the Yom Kippur War, that meant finally completing a long-term strategy of normalization. Those pressures were harshly intensified as the FRG was scheduled to take the presidency of the Council of the European Community since January 1974, where it might be expected to promote the concept of the indivisibility of détente. This meant extending to the whole Mediterranean area the same kind of East-West understandings that were being elaborated within the framework of the preparatory phase of the Conference on Security and Cooperation in Europe (CSCE). As we have noticed, that might be perceived as a general mood of European politics in those days, as it was also reflected through an increasingly shared attitude between the center-left majority and the communist opposition in the Italian parliament on such issues.

Kissinger's view was quite opposed to such an idea. On January 25, 1974, he explicitly said as much while briefing the NATO ambassadors in Brussels. That is, far from envisaging any kind of Soviet-American condominium in the Middle East, US policy of cooperation with Moscow was precisely aimed at preventing any excessive Soviet influence in that region—that is, no more than a kind of a new-style, and possibly good-mannered, containment policy. Cooperation would be hampered if Moscow would insist on "extreme" demands—which in his view, would not mean anything more than fostering any "too intense pace in the elaboration of a peace settlement." More importantly, in order to clarify this to who was expected to understand it in the first place, Kissinger also specified that "a precise knowledge of that would also facilitate a correct appreciation of American-Soviet cooperation *in other areas* [italics added]."[20] In other words, West German politicians were now being warned to refrain from whatever further diplomatic move toward Moscow that would not have been previously authorized from Washington. Too much was at stake on a global scale—i.e., the Middle East—to admit whatever distinction might be made between a global—i. e. American—and a regional concept of détente.

US NATO Ambassador Donald Rumsfeld had already anticipated as much when he told his colleagues in Brussels on October 16, 1973, that even western participation in CSCE should no longer be taken for granted.[21] This meant that the US was no longer prepared to leave West Germany—or any other western European partner—with any autonomous role with regard to European aspects of the détente processes. Least of all now when some European NATO allies might put forth initiatives which might be not fully consistent with US global strategy. The Declaration issued by the nine EC countries on November 6th—which demanded recognition of UN Resolution 242 on the Arab-Israeli conflict, and mentioned the "legitimate rights" of the Palestinian people—was a case in point.

Kissinger was also becoming less reluctant to consider some kind of active interference in West German politics. In mid-October he received the conservative opposition leader Franz-Joseph Strauss for face-to-face talks. After the meeting, Strauss had been quick to call German journalists in Washington to a press conference where he warned them about the bitter American uneasiness with European behavior. Of course, Ambassador von Staden was informed about the talk, and he reported to Bonn without any comment that Kissinger's actual words had been far less diplomatic—as he had mentioned allegations ranging from lack of responsibility to unfitness for partnership.[22]

Such pressure might be viewed in Bonn—where party and coalition politics has also become increasingly strained during that winter—as taking unpredictable risks in German-American relations. Whatever the motives, Brandt reacted by lowering the profile of his foreign policy initiative—which had just reached a peak as he had protested against US use of West German facilities for arms supplies to Israel during the Yom Kippur War—even though he had not changed his mind on the issues.

As to his own beliefs, Brandt was still quite outspoken to Israeli Prime Minister Golda Meir during a summit meeting of the Socialist International that was held in London on November 16, 1973—on Meir's request. Meir had solicited that meeting precisely in order to assail the EC Middle East Declaration on ideological grounds. On that occasion, she compared Israel's situation to what had been Spain's in 1936 and Czechoslovakia's in 1938. While British Prime Minister Harold Wilson had supported Meir's views, Brandt had firmly countered that, rather, the EC declaration involved a European commitment to the security of Israel grounded on a much more realistic basis then Meir had conceived and one that would serve both Europe's unity and the interests of the Middle East as keenly associated to Western Europe's.[23]

Promoting a strict association between the Middle East and Western Europe, as Brandt was suggesting, would mean no less than an overt confrontation with the whole set of current US policies at the time. Yet, no such confrontation took place. There is no sufficient evidence to illustrate why Brandt finally chose to downplay those issues during the following months, until the famous spy scandal compelled him to leave office in May 1974. Indeed, his position inside his own party and his coalition government was faltering.[24] Finance Minister Helmut Schmidt, who was known as the most committed champion of a strict alignment to American political leadership inside the NATO alliance, was left the opportunity of exerting a leading role regarding German participation in the Washington energy conference in early February 1974, where he virtually outflanked Foreign Minister Scheel himself.[25]

It is noticeable that Schmidt was quick to cable Bonn—without any comment—how Kissinger would see any further European-Arab dialogue on oil and security issues as a "backstab to his own peace efforts", and how that should be "taken seriously."[26] Whether or not Schmidt might have obtained any distinct information thereof—discussions inside the White House about how to handle the Europeans were serious enough. The official wording of the threatened countermeasures to any European ally allegedly displaying unloyal behavior was centered on the concept of a major troop removal that would leave it helpless in the face of Soviet greed. Actually more realistic scenarios were being considered in Washington behind the scenes: namely, dramatically lowering the nuclear threshold in case of any severe military confrontation with the Soviet Union and being ready to fight it out to the last European city. "Right now", Kissinger argued just on the eve of the Washington energy conference, "if a war started in Europe, within five days, we would be in a nuclear war. If we started pulling our forces out, the argument is that Europe would go neutralist. If they are going that way anyway, we could leave the trip wire and go nuclear like we would have to do anyway. Our forces give Europe the security to bitch at us." Besides, Kissinger also admitted, as American troops were there precisely in order to prevent any neutralist development in western Europe, just a few would suffice to do that job.[27]

On the other hand, just while those pressures were at a peak, as Brandt's closest aide and most trusted negotiator Egon Bahr was back from Moscow by the end of March, he might bring home some level of warm encouragement—yet no effective Soviet commitment on Berlin-related issues that might soften East German stubbornness.[28] At first glance, that might support the view that the main ambitions of Brandt's and Bahr's *Ostpolitik* were already doomed—whatever might have happened in the Middle East—just because of Moscow's choice to give absolute priority to relations with Washington in order to ensure, at least, that Soviet control of Eastern Europe would not be questioned.[29] More recent studies, based on Soviet sources, have shown a more complex pattern, characterized by a high degree of uncertainty and inner debate in Moscow.[30] Actually, the contents of Bahr's interview with Brezhnev in late March were at least double-faced. Brezhnev had gone out of his way in order to express his full solidarity with Brandt in spite of the latter's current "personal and political difficulties", and to confirm that his own interest for cooperation with Bonn, far from diminishing, was even increased after the settlement of the postwar European borders; he even went so far as admitting that the freedom of expression and open cultural exchanges were no longer a forbidden subject, and that he did not see why foreign radio transmissions should continue to be blocked in the Soviet Union.

The mood, however, had suddenly changed as soon as Bahr had mentioned the Berlin situation as the key issue where all those promising ideas most needed to be translated into facts, whatever the East German leaders might think—and it was known that the latter's opinion about Brandt was opposite to Brezhnev's. Clearly enough, Brezhnev might not be able to run any risk on the most sensitive issues of Soviet policy about Germany—however unwillingly—while he was being assailed at home about how Soviet moderation had actually paid off in the Middle East. After all, putting Berlin at risk had already been paid for very bitterly by many a previous Soviet leader inside the Kremlin.[31]

However little successful, Bahr's mission to Moscow was implicitly also a target of NATO Secretary General Joseph Luns' sharp criticism of Germany's "reticent" way of practicing consultation inside the alliance. As German NATO Ambassador Krapf reported to Bonn on May 2nd, any declaration of the West German government about their Atlantic commitment would be worthless if they would not "pay more attention than before to the specific value of consultation inside the alliance", and if they would not give more "substantial" and more "timely" contributions. It was clearly specified that this criticism was about the whole set of current world issues, including the European ones—which meant that the way the Warsaw Pact countries should be dealt with was no longer within the realm of German competence to any significant extent. Strangely enough, Krapf was referring Luns' views to his government together with his own comment, which qualified them as quite "grounded"—a clear sign of Brandt's growing isolation in Bonn.[32] When Brandt's close aide Günther Guillaume was suddenly "unveiled" as an East German agent just a few days later, the right opportunity was given to his foreign and domestic critics. His most credible long-time political rival inside his party was perfectly prepared to seize it.

Historians may not be expected to say anything indisputable on subjects too close to spy stories—nor should they even try. However, Brandt's resignation in May 1974 can not be understood without reference to such a framework, one that was determined by those processes. Anyway, as Schmidt finally took office as the new West German chancellor, the mood of US-West German relations was changed almost overnight. "Schmidt has none of Brandt's rapid sentimentality", Kissinger briefed some Congressmen at the White House shortly after. "Where a year ago they [i. e. the Germans] thought we needed them, now that has changed. *In the Middle East they see we are right* [italics added] and we are urging them to move on the economics as long as it is supportive."[33]

Of course, mentioning the Middle East *and* the economy was not just another way to look at the agenda. It meant mentioning the two most intimately connected issues that would influence the fate of mankind until well into the next century. As the huge amount of dollar balances that had been dangling over the world economy during the few previous years had shifted away from Western European to mainly conservative Arab treasuries—where they might be expected to be far safer—a master card might be played on behalf of the American set of stakes that was represented by the Nixon administration—and of all compatible ones throughout the world.

Two different paths were open. On the one hand, a multilateral approach might be undertaken to set priorities and to discover the tools in order to reach some new kind of equilibrium between surplus and deficit situations on a world scale. Originally, both the IMF and the World Bank did favor that approach, as they took the oil crisis for one more reason to pursue a general reform of the monetary system, rather than to slow down that process. On the other hand, formerly favored special interests might agree among themselves in the first place, as well as with the special power goals that were being fixed as US goals by the Nixon administration, in order to arrange things according to their wishes and needs.

The Nixon administration did not conceal its inclination to favor the latter choice. On the eve of the Washington Energy Conference, an aide-mémoire of the Office of the Assistant [Treasury] Secretary for International Affairs (OASIA) stated clearly that optimizing the effects of the global investments of oil income should involve no new rules nor any new institutional machinery: rather, market forces should be relied upon in order to reach optimum allocation.[34]

Nixon administration officials were rather inclined to take the dollar and oil crisis as an opportunity to change the IMF's and the World Bank's roles, and to shift them from controlling and even influencing world market forces—as they were meant to be doing according to the Bretton Woods New Dealist philosophy —into just acting as the latters' agencies. That policy was firmly established while the oil crisis was under way—as it was being planned during Saudi-Egyptian talks that were conducted by Saudi officials with deep-rooted US connections.[35] As concerned the international financial institutions (IFI's), Assistant Treasury Secretary John Hennessy briefed the US National Advisory Council on International Financial Policies (NAC) on April 20, 1973, that the private sector did not believe they were "of much help to them," and was said to fulfil their view as he argued that the International Finance Corporation—an agency inside the World Bank that had been created in 1956 to promote shareholding on the part of private banking business—"could provide greater help."[36]

By then, German officials were not yet fully convinced. As late as October

1974, Bundesbank Deputy Governor Otmar Emminger expressed his preference for multilateral governance of any financial re-adjustment process through some kind of "international government agency for the investment of oil surpluses."[37] A few days before, the newly appointed West German Finance Minister Hans Apel—who was known as a moderate-wing member of SPD—had addressed the annual assembly of the World Bank about the need to prevent banking activities from flowing into destinations governed by weak credit controls in order to escape public supervision.[38]

However, both were being outflanked through Schmidt's firm decision to identify German national interest with the artful restoration of a dollar standard. This maneuver was being operated through unofficial consent inside the international financial community while international banking and currency-market deregulation continued.[39] Just few weeks after Schmidt had taken office as the new West German Chancellor, an OASIA report appreciated him as "much more pragmatic about the potential of EC unity", and predicted that German officials would now show themselves even more eager to "earn interests on dollar reserves", rather than still encouraging any attempt to promote any wholesome monetary reform.[40]

Ruling out whatever kind of any publicly negotiated institutional reform of the international monetary system was indeed one fundamental choice on which a newly emerging Atlantic or "trilateral" consent was going to be based. Such an idea would rest upon three pillars. First, the acknowledgement of the special role of the dollar in spite of whatever might make that role appear to be doubtful;[41] second, a general relaxation of all existing practices and rules that enabled governments to exert political or even legal supervision on money flows across the world; third, a silent and yet very effective transfer of decision powers in this field from institutional and publicly accountable seats into some informal and mainly privately-based ones.

On this basis, the Chancellor might confidently tell a re-emerging Deng Xiaoping upon his visit to Beijng in late October 1975 that German dollar purchases had reached such a peak that the FRG was now holding more dollar reserves than the United States, the Soviet Union, Canada, and others, put together.[42] Schmidt, of course, also admitted to be fully aware that the role of the dollar as a functioning measure of values" was nothing more than a "traditional convention"—whereas "it actually might not be." However, as he told Deputy Foreign Minister Hans-Jürgen Wischnewski on June 6, 1975, he mistrusted whatever alternative approach as possibly leading to further disturbances. "Once one 'goes out' of the dollar—which might happen out of merely political reasons—there might be an increased unsettlement of the world economic system."[43] According to Schmidt, reaching a breackthrough from the world crisis involved excluding two factors that he saw as generating unrest and ineffectiveness: talks about any "general" reform, and publicity of debates at a decision-making level—as the latter would disturb the work of skilled and well-trained hands. This was precisely what the Trilateral Commission promoted, which Schmidt wholeheartedly supported. After the Franco-American reconciliation worked out through the Martinique meeting between Gerald Ford and Valéry Giscard d'Estaing—he told Wishnewski,

> I conceived that, in the second half of January, a group of no more than fifteen people should gather for two or three days, with no publicity (and, possibly, anonymously) in such a big city like Hamburg, Munich, or Frankfurt. The German side should entrust itself with invitations and preparations. It should not be a meeting of officials but of people who enjoy the confidence of their government.[44]

So, whereas the shadow of a serious cross-Atlantic confrontation had shaped the climate in early 1974, with a peak during the Washington energy conference, Kissinger's and Schmidt's political victory in that framework was now evolving into the establishment of a new rigid Atlantic consensus —"trilaterally" extended to an active involvement of Japan—on just the three pillars that have been mentioned above. Pompidou's death had paved the way for a Franco-American reapproachment in terms of France's active role to promote that program under a leadership—like Giscard's—which had never been so deeply rooted within the ranks of the same international financial community that was sponsoring it.

That was the meaning of the appointment that was scheduled at Rambouillet for November 15, 1975, with Giscard as a guest. Ford and Kissinger went there with the explicit aim of finalizing the delegitimation of whatever surviving thought there might be about any general reform of the world economy. Indeed such a will was firmly established inside the administration. The memorandum that Ford had received by his assistant for economic affairs, William Seidman, shortly before leaving to Rambouillet, sounded like a far-reaching and committing manifesto. "At this point"—it stated, in a style that might sound unfit to address a president—we believe it is important for you to focus on the principles on which our strategy in the international arena is founded."

Of these, the first one was a refusal of any concept of a new international order. All such ideas were contemptuously characterized as "based on socialist principles", so that any such thing "would require us to either (a) become socialist or quasi-socialist, or (b) become economically isolationist." The President was presented with a choice between making a preliminary declaration of principle in favor of "free enterprise" moderated by some ritual openness to discuss problems on a co-operative basis, or, inversely, adopting an initially open attitude which would be followed by actual firmness on any specific issue. The former was to be chosen:

We believe that our interests can only be served by speaking out frankly and forth-rightly concerning our basic disagreement in principle with those who are demanding a new economic order. The principles of free market and free enterprise are, after all, what we stand for and what we believe in. If we fail to speak out in their defense, no one else will be able to do so.

That meant all "pressures" by Third World countries for international agreements on non-energy commodity prices:

If we posture ourselves as willing to discuss this area, with an eye towards "new solutions" or "new arrangements", the world will perceive this as a willingness on our part to compromise our basic system. In any statement referring to discussions on this issue, we should not be afraid to strongly assert that the United States, as well as the less fortunate countries, can best be served not by a system of government agreements on various aspects of international trade and finance, but rather by continued reliance on the effective private institutions that have evolved in these areas.[45]

The official proceedings of the Rambouillet summit meeting eventually furnished those bare concepts with a convenient amount of window-dressing about the need for co-operation and the condemnation of trade barriers. Because of this, few authors choose to present that summit as itself representing a significant turning point[46]—although it was the first of an unbroken series of annual economic summit conferences among the same countries. Actually, very little was added to a set of basic choices that were to influence the global framework of world civilization for decades to come: these were already at work, and were little more than tacitly confirmed at Rambouillet. That was also why Italian Prime Minister Aldo Moro—who was known for his leaning toward enabling the Italian Communists to share responsibilities in the country's problems—was significantly out of tune as he proposed that "countries with state-administered foreign trade" be solicited to join international economic or financial institutions, from which, with the exception of Romania, they were being still excluded.[47] There seems to be no record that any of those present paid any attention to Moro's proposal. Besides, it may hardly be supposed that anybody inside the Soviet state and party bureaucracy would have appreciated hearing such ideas. Nor would they have likely sounded more appealing to most of the Italian communist party bureaucracy itself—where the prevailing economic thinking was still based on some offhand injections short-term pragmatic appreciations of a fundamentally doctrinaire background, which made Berlinguer's far-sighted perceptions somewhat peculiar.[48]

But, finally, it was left to Schmidt to capture the core significance of the Rambouillet meeting. Indeed, the minutes for the German Foreign Ministry record that the Chancellor fostered the summit to publicly place strong emphasis on one concept, so that everybody would finally hear:

> [... One has to] make it clear before world public opinion that a phase of world recession is no fitting time to pursue any "new economic order"; the question is just about improving the structure of the global outlook of the functions of world economy.[49]

The American delegation at Rambouillet might embrace the feeling that the spirit of the Seidman memo was fully shared by a nominally socialist West German Chancellor. The political and personal confidence that had grown between Kissinger and Schmidt might also suggest that the latter would not object to a very important principle that the Seidman memo also stated as a consequence of its prescriptions: that is, that national sovereignties should be strictly limited as regarded internal policies in the main Western countries—whatever people like Aldo Moro might think:

> [...] If we agree, or give the appearance to agree, to changes in the international economic system abroad, we will be in danger of jeopardizing the principles you have been building at home, and our economic and military strength will increasingly count for less in the world.[50]

On that ground, while the Italian communist party leader Enrico Berlinguer might appear to have in mind the West German model as he fostered a new bipartisan consent about Italy's foreign policy choices—including NATO membership—he was hopelessly outflanked through the sudden shift in West German attitudes that went on since May 1974. That meant economic no less than security matters—namely, Mediterranean and Middle Eastern. Indeed, both dimensions were deeply intermingled.

By December 1974—as Berlinguer presented that platform to the party's central committee while preparing the impending party congress—events ecclipsed Berlinguer's novel approach. Perhaps he was somewhat aware of those difficulties, as he would not repeat before the opening of the party congress what he dared to say to his colleagues in private about what he meant: namely, that "a great peace and progress goal" should now be nothing less than a "step by step unification of the world market", which also meant pursuing "a monetary system that would be valid for relations among all countries."[51]

Had these matters still been relevant in international politics, such words meant as deep a breakaway from the Soviet experience as might be made by any political party that was still named communist. That would have meant choosing a way to break ties with the Soviet Union that was both the most radical and the most responsible—because it did not foreclose on any deep-reaching pragmatic understandings.

Though, just that kind of emancipation was also the least acceptable to Berlinguer's actual or potential interlocutors at the head of the main western countries. Berlinguer was simply echoing a Rooseveltian "one world" idea in a Nixonian and Kissingerian context. That was why he appeared to be so dangerous.

During Italian President Giovanni Leone's and Prime Minister Aldo Moro's visit to Washington in September 1974, Kissinger explained that a responsible communist party was more dangerous than an irresponsible one, because "if they appear to be responsible they will be a bigger threat in the long run." Of course, this was either a truism, or nonsense. Yet Kissinger did know it as a fact, and was unshaken: during a break, he confidentially briefed President Ford on the importance of being tautologous by showing him the dangers of any communist power-sharing in Rome, even if Soviet-styled dictatorships were not to be involved. "The problem with Italy", he said, "is that with communists in government—they would be competent—it would make them irresistible in France, isolate Germany, give Papandreu an opening in Greece. The *socialists* [italics added] never would have gained power in Germany if that nice idiot hadn't taken them into a coalition. That makes them respectable. *The same would happen in Italy* [italics added]."[52] But it was not Germany's isolation that he meant. It was just Helmut Schmidt's. Risking any revival of Brandt's and Bahr's policies on a continental scale was simply too much.

1. See Andrew J. Rotter, "Christians, Muslims, and Hindus: Religion and US-South Asian Relations, 1947–1954", *Diplomatic History*, Vol. 24 (2000), pp. 593-616.

2. Nixon himself put that issue very outspokenly to his Cabinet in terms of a sharp reversal of the very vision that had been underlying such things as the Marshall Plan, inter alia. "The United States", he said shortly after the Yom Kippur War and the oil shock, "should move away from multilateral to bilateral aid [...] We need it for foreign policy

[...] The IMF sort of thing is OK, but we need this tool for our foreign policy. This is to be closely held, because it goes against the grain of the altruists [...] The World Bank does a fine job, but it is not an effective instrument of US policy. Frequently, it has not helped where we wanted and it has helped countries where it was not in our interest [...] We must be strong not just in order to be number one but because it is essential for own diplomacy with *the Soviet Union, Europe and the rest* [italics added]. If they get the impression that the US is turning away from world leadership, we are finished." US UN Ambassador John Scali, who also attended the meeting, might have felt concerned that he was seen as a possible "altruist", and advanced some cautious objections. National Archives And Record Administration (NARA), Gerald R. Ford Presidential Library (GFPL), *National Security Adviser Memoranda of Conversations 1973-1977 (NSA Memoranda)*, Box 4, May 28th 1974 Cabinet Meeting.

3. Friedrich-Ebert-Stiftung (FES), *Archiv der sozialen Demokratie (ASD), Depositum Bahr*, Mappe 1, Ordner 436: Werner D. Lippert, *Richard Nixon's Détente and Willy Brandt's Ostpolitik: The Political and Ecomomic Diplomacy of Engaging with the East*, Ph. D. Dissertation, Graduate School of Vanderbilt University, Nashville, Tennesse, August 2005, p. 189. ["Europas Gewicht wächst in dem Masse, in dem die relative Bedeutung der Sicherheitsfrage geringer wird. Wir haben in den letzten Jahren aktiv daran mitgewirkt, die beiden Supermächte anzuannähern und sie damit politisch relativ manipulierbar gemacht, wie sie militärisch überhaupt nicht sind"].

4. See Enzo Collotti, *Dalle due Germanie alla Germania unita.* (Turin: Einaudi, 1992), pp. 43ff..

5. See Vladimir Falin, *Politische Erinnerungen.* (Munich: Dromer Knaur,1994), *passim*.

6. East Germans suspicions and negative pressures about whatever hint at some understandings there might be between the Soviet Union and the FRG—as well as those coming from Warsaw and Prague—were indeed deeply rooted. In fact, those processes seem to have significantly contributed to Khrushchev's downfall. On that, see Douglas Selvage, *The Warsaw Pact and Nuclear Nonproliferation, 1963-1965*, CWIHP Working Paper No. 32: http://cwihp.si.edu; see also O. Bange, already q., pp. 1-12;

7. In a report to Brandt on July 30th 1973, short before a Warsaw Pact summit that would actually issue some strikingly stubborn statements about West German current policies: FES, *ASD, Depositum Bahr*, Mappe 2, Ordner 432: W. D. Lippert, *op. cit.*, p. 189.

8. Kissinger's mistrust was unshaken. "Egon Bahr", he told National Security Adviser Brent Scowcroft, Defense Secretary Schlesinger, and the latter's military aide, General Wickham, while briefing them on September 5th 1973, "would like to get our support for a neutral united Germany, and then send us away": NARA, GPFL; *NSA*, Box 2.

9. On that, see mainly H. J. Laub, *The Development of the Israeli-Egyptian- American Relationship from the Death of Egyptian President Gamal Abdel Nasser in September*

*1970 to the Camp David Agreements in September 1978* (London: Minerva Press, 1998); G. W. Breslauer, *Soviet Strategy in The Middle East* (Boston: Unwin Hyman, 1990); William Bundy, *A Tangled Web. The Making of Foreign Policy in the Nixon Presidency* (New York: Hill and Wang, 1998); R. Garthoff, *Détente and Confrontation, American-Soviet Relations from Nixon to Reagan* (Washington DC: Brooking Institution Press,1994;) F. Logevall, A. Preston, *Nixon in the World. American Foreign Relations, 1969-1977* (Oxford/New York: Oxford University Press, 2008).

10. NARA, GFPL, *NSA Memoranda,* Box 2.

11. *Ibidem* (The Pentagon, September 5th 1973: Kissinger Schlesinger – Wickham – Scowcroft). The transcript of Kissinger's words spells: "We want the Egyptians where we were with the RDV—we have to get the thing past an unconditional surrender." It may be noticed that these words are only present in the original minutes, whereas the corresponding passage is canceled with black ink in the taped version of the same transcript. It may also be added that Kissinger admitted much more than he does in his memoirs while briefing the new President Gerald L. Ford on the Middle Eastern situation as late as August 1974. See *Ibidem,* Box 4: Memorandum of Conversation, August 12th 1974 (Ford, Kissinger, Scowcroft: The Oval Office) ["*Secretary Kissinger*: We didn't expect the October War. *The President*: But wasn't it helpful? *Secretary Kissinger*: We couldn't have done better if we had set the scenario. *The President*: Even the heavy Israeli losses helped, didn't they? *Secretary Kissinger*: Once the war started, we helped Israel stabilize the situation. But it was not without a cost they couldn't sustain. [...The war] reversed some Arab cockiness— But the Arabs know Israel can't stand attrition."]

12. *Ibidem,* Box 4: Memorandum of Conversation: President- Members of theCabinet-Scowcroft (March 8th 1974).

13. *Ibidem*: Cabinet meeting June 21st 1974.

14. *Ibidem*: Cabinet meeting, June 20th 1974.

15."I am doing something but I can't surface it now", Kissinger told Defense Secretary Schlesinger, National Security Adviser Scowcroft and General Wickham at the Pentagon just one month before the Yon Kippur War, on September 5th 1973. That was just when he stated his sympathetic comparison between Sadat's situation with Israel and his own to North Vietnam: see Ref. 38.

16. It was Israeli Ambassador Simcha Dinitz who raised that issue, soon after he felt encouraged by Kissinger's report on how Brezhnev's efforts had been dealt with in San Clemente. "*Dinitz:* I have a few more points. The Prime Minister [Golda Meir], subsequent to Brandt's visit, said he [i. e. Brandt] sent a letter to Nixon and to Brezhnev talking of his impression of Israel's desire of peace. [...] She wanted the President to know this [...] When those people come to Israel they talk differently [...] Talking to the British deputy foreign minister he said to someone that Israel was responsible for the Six Days' War.—*Kissinger*: I don't remember the contents, but Brandt is not noted for his precision

of thought.—*Dinitz*: We will try to influence the German government if you don't object. —*Kissinger*: No. We will too." NARA, GFPL, *NSA Memoranda,* Box 2.

17. *Akten zur auswärtigen Politik der Bundesrepublik Deutschland* [henceforth, *ADAP*], *1974,* Band I, p. 31 ff.

18. As Brandt had given a revealing interview to the Italian communist newspaper *Paese Sera* as early as January 1969, where he had also stated his intention to break the Grand Coalition and to call for early elections, he received a journalist of the same newspaper soon after his appointment as Chancellor for a confidential talk, and the latter reported to party secretary Luigi Longo in Rome his impression that the new socialist chancellor intended to upgrade the dialogue between the two parties (Note for Comrade Luigi Longo from Giorgio Signorini, received on October 29, 1969: Fondazione Istituto Gramsci, Rome: *Archivio del Partito Comunista Italiano,* 1969, microfilm 0308, p. 1326).

19. That inference was cautiously hinted at in a letter of 30 December 1969 where Leo Bauer, who was Brandt's personal ambassador to the Italian communists, told the head of the PCI's foreign department, Sergio Segre, that contacts should be almost frozen because of the "difficulties" that might be foreseen in both countries after the recent dramatic developments in Italy: *FES, ASD,* Nachlass Leo Bauer, Box 10: R. D'Agata, "Il contesto europeo della distensione internazionale", in Agostino Giovagnoli, Silvio Pons (a cura di), *L'Italia repubblicana nella crisi degli anni settanta,* Vol. I, *Tra guerra fredda e distensione* (Soveria Mannelli: Rubbettino, 2004), p. 315 and Ref.

20. Ambassador von Staden, Washington, to the Auswärtiges Amt, 25. 1. 1974: *Akten zur Auswärtigen Politik der Bundesrepublik Deutschland (ADAP), 1974,* Band 1., p. 94. "The Soviet Union", Nixon would tell Kissinger and Scowcroft just a few days later, "wanted that each of us would send a couple of divisions [to the Middle East]. We said no. They said: 'We'll go alone'. Then we went on alarm" (NARA, GPFL, *NSA Memoranda,* Box 4: Cabinet, Kissinger, Scowcroft, March 8th 1974).

21. *ADAP 1973,* Band 3, p. 1568.

22. Ambassador von Staden to the State Secretary of the West German Foreign Ministry, Paul Frank: *ADAP, 1973,* III, pp. 332 ss.

23. *ASD, Depositum Eppler,* 1/EEA0000. Brandt's views were shared by Palme, Kreisky, and De Martino—but not by Harold Wilson.

24. The most recent reconstruction of the political origins of Brandt's downfall openly describes it as much more the outcome of an internal political game than of an international one, as the relatively insignificant Günther Guillaume had transmitted much less information to East Berlin than many lower-level agents in several Bonn ministries were normally doing, and the curiously belated 'discovery' was clearly orchestrated: see Carole Fink, Bernd Schaeffer (eds.), *Ostpolitik 1969-1974: European and Global Responses*: Publications of the German Historical Institute (Cambridge, UK: Cambridge

University Press, 2009); also see Hermann Schreiber, *Kanzlersturz: Warum Willy Brandt zurücktrat* (Düsseldorf: Econ, 2003).

25. Nixon was probably meaning just Schmidt as he briefed Finance Secretary Shultz on the importance of "talking pork" with the "technical types" during the conference: NARA, GFL; *NSA Memoranda,* Box 4: Nixon, Kissinger, Schultz, Simon, Scowcroft, Februray 9th 1974.

26. *ASD, Willy-Brandt* Archiv [*WBA*], Mappe 18: D'Agata, "Il contesto...", cit., p. 24.

27. "We've got to define the question. We keep our forces there, so they won't go neutralist. If we withdraw half our troops, how will they behave differently? I don't suggest troop withdrawal now, but honestly we don't need all these forces": Memorandum of Conversation: Nixon, Kissinger, Shultz, Simon, Scowcroft, February 9th 1974: *NSA, GFL,* Box 4. One month later, relations with Europe were discussed at the White House even more scrupulessly: see *NARA, GFL, NSA Memoranda,* Box 4: Cabinet, Kissinger, Scowcroft, March 8th 1974. [*Secretary Kssinger:* Europe is organizing overall on an anti-American basis. *The President:* They can have Africa—we will take South Africa and get out of the UN. Why does State hate South Africa? *Secretary Kissinger:* I have abolished the Political Science Division in State. *The President:* I noticed the Lamizana coup. They can hardly wait for the New York Times editorial—like in Greece. *Secretary Kissinger:* Look at Amin. He used to be ours, and the Kenyans bought him"].

28. *ADAP 1974*, I, p. 241 ff.

29. See Werner D. Lippert, *Richard Nixon's Détente and Willy Brandt's Ostpolitik: The Political and Ecomomic Diplomacy of Engaging with the East* (Ph. D. Dissertation, Graduate School of Vanderbilt University, Nashville, Tennesse, August 2005), p. 208. According to that reconstruction, a "conservative" shift would have taken place inside the Politburo after the fulfillment of the treaties with Bonn about European borders, which would have made useless any further development of relations with Bonn.

30. See Andrey Edemskiy, "Dealing with Bonn: Leonid Brezhnev and the Soviet Response to German *Ostpolitik*", in Carole Fink, Bernd Schaeffer (eds.), already q., pp. 15-38.

31. See above, Ref. 28.

32. *ADAP 1974,* Band 1., p. 141.

33. *NARA, GFPL, NSA Memoranda,* Box 3.

34. NARA, *RG 56,* Entry 171, Box 2: "The Roosa Paper and the US Approach", February 2th 1974. The motive for this comment was criticism of a proposal by the former Treasury Assistant Secretary in the Kennedy Administration, Robert Roosa, which pleaded for an OPEC fund for government securities and an OPEC mutual investment trust. The trust should be aimed at promoting additional investment in oil-consuming

countries in order to prevent the loss of real income from causing a severe slowdown. In order to guard against exchange losses, OPEC subscription should be designated in terms of a market basket of currencies. Moreover, different mutual investment trusts were proposed for different specific purposes, and percentage limits were envisaged for holdings in any given country or company.

35. See William Bundy, *A Tangled Web. The Making of the Foreign Policy in the Nixon Presidency* (New York: Hill & Wang, 1999), pp. 433-4.

36. NARA, *RG 56*, Entry 15-19, Box 1.

37. Address by Otmar Emminger, Deputy Governor of the Deutsche Bundesbank, at the Bank of Spain, Madrid, October 14th 1974: Auswärtiges Amt, *Politisches Archiv, Zwischenarchiv*, 117102.

38. Ibidem.

39. The link between financial deregulation and the international role of the dollar was very clear to US policy-makers and officials. Less than two years after the oil shock, US Deputy Treasury Secretary Bennett explained to the OCDE Economic Policy Committee that "the dollar had shown lesser instability over the last two years than number of other currencies." Bennett, the record continues, "noted number of factors relevant to function of the dollar: (a) US encouraging OPEC to continue to invest in dollars in US (through bilateral conversations, *administration opposition to legislation calling for screening* [italics added] and no intention of imposing capital controls; (b) some improvement in outlook for political stability in the Middle East; (c) US lead in downward trend of interest rates ending and rates likely to turn up in future as domestic demand strengthens; (d) residual effect of past devaluations still working through system; (e) better US performance on inflation than most other countries." *NARA*, RG56, Entry 171, Box 2: Meeting of the OCDE Economic Policy Committee, Paris, March 5th 1973.

40. OASIA Briefing for Simon's visit to Europe, July 1974: *NARA, RG 56*, Entry 171, Box 1.

41. Although the early euphoria that soon followed the oil shock was contradicted by some news about oil incomes migrating to the Deutschemark or to the yen during the early months of 1975, Nixon administration officials did not worry much. For instance, a FED minute directed to its president, Arthur Burns, quietly stated that, should the flow of Arab funds "be directed in very large amounts to a particular foreign country [...], that country might have a serious problem. For instance, if Arab owners of euro-dollars were to decide to shift them into DM; the German authorities would face the possibility of excessive liquidity at home." (NARA, GFPL, *Burns Papers*, B86).

42. *AAPD 1975*, II, p. 1491.

43. *AAPD 1975*, I, p. 809.

44. Ibidem.

45. NARA, GFPL, *Seidman Papers*, Box 137.

46. For an exception, see Harold James, *Rambouillet 15 November 1975: Die Globalisierung der Wirtschaft* (Munich: DTV, 1997).

47. *ADAP 1975*, II, p. 1652.

48. On that, see Luciano Barca, *Cronache dall'interno del PCI* (Soveria Mannelli: Rubbettino, 1975), Vol. II, *passim*.

49. *ADAP 1975*, II, 1648. ["Er wolle einen starken Ton der Entschiedenheit öffentlich hörbar machen [...man müsse] der Weltöffentlichkeit gegenüber ausdrücken, daß Phase einer Weltrezession kein günstiger Zeitpunkt für die Herbeiführung einer 'neuen wirtschaftsordnung' ist; es gehe um die Verbesserung der Struktur der weltwirtschaftlichen Funktionszusammenhänge"].

50. See Ref. 45.

51. Enrico Berlinguer, *La proposta comunista. Relazione al Comitato centrale e alla Commissione centrale di controllo del Partito comunista italiano in preparazione del XIV Congresso* (Turin: Einaudi, 1975), pp. 56-7.

52. NARA, GFPL, *NSA Memoranda,* Box 6.

*Lawrence Gray*

# An Uneasy Empire:
# Myth, Obsession, Identity and American Policy

It is interesting to compare what actually happened during the Cold War years with what could have happened. My paper will look at the legacy of the Cold War: the end of a bipolar system and the emergence of a unipolar order where the United States has been largely unchecked in its efforts to run the world. What may be the costs and consequences of this legacy for the administration of Barack Obama?

Westad raises a fundamental point about junior officials of one generation of Soviet leaders rising to replace the preceding generation only to find themselves the architects of a completely different paradigm. This makes us wonder about Obama's advisors given that they were junior players in previous administrations, notably Clinton's. And there is a further consideration. An underlying problem is that Russian experts in the US have been replaced by the post-Cold War generation, now grown to maturity and authority. If the Cold Warriors were forged in the 1960s, the post-Cold Warriors are forever mired in the 1990s.[1] And Obama's key advisers on Russia share something with those who advised George W. Bush: their view of Russia grew out of the 1990s.

These experts believe that the 1990s represented a stable platform from which to reform Russia, that the grumbling of Russians plunged into poverty and international irrelevancy at that time was simply part of the post-Cold War order. They believe that without economic power, Russia could not be an important player on the international stage. Therefore, they expected Russia to revert to its 1990s patterns.[2]

What was the effect of the Cold War on American influence in the post-Cold War years? The Cold War perpetuated and strengthened long-standing self-perceptions of exceptionalism among the American people. American nationalism, as well as the American approach to politics in general prior to World War II, was a product of domestic experiences and values that were developed in isolation from the international state-system, notably the European state-system.

From the very beginning of their national life Americans believed strongly in their destiny: to bring freedom and social justice to all men. The massive immigration of the nineteenth century seemed to reinforce this sense of destiny. The American writer John Dos Passos observed "the repudiation of Europe is, after all, America's main excuse for being." After World War II the United States confronted the world with beliefs  and behavior patterns inherited from a long period of isolation from Europe.[3]

*From World War to Cold War*

After the end of the Cold War, the 1990s were a boom decade and while the economies began crashing at the beginning of 2000 it was 9/11 that ushered in a new era, where unexpected changes occurred. This new era has an historical parallel. The situation that the Americans faced in 1944 was entirely new. A perceived need to contain the Soviet Union by establishing and maintaining a balance of power required long-range policies that would combine all the factors of power.[4] This need ran contrary to the expectations of the American people when, after 1945, they wanted to return to a way of life they had before the war. It remained to be seen, of course, whether an impatient people, an inward-looking nation, without experience in international politics, could adjust to the demands of power politics.[5]

The United States was led by a man who never expected to be president and he led Americans to where they never expected to be taken. Under Harry Truman the US moved through the Truman Doctrine, the Marshall Plan, the Berlin Airlift, NATO, Containment, and the onset of the Cold War—unimaginable events if seen from the perspective of the war-time alliance with the Soviet Union. It was far from anyone's imagination in 1945 or even 1947 that what had happened by the end of the decade of the 1940s would happen. Truman was only supposed to bring the troops home. No one expected Truman (least of all himself) would be a president who would be remembered for his bold actions.[6]

It would be words rather than deeds that were daring during the ensuing Cold War years. There is more than a fair chance that the pre-1989 East European regimes would still be around today if the events of that year had not occurred. Yet it is unlikely the East European countries would have reformed from within. Clearly the US missed an opportunity during the early part of 1989 in not pressing for more agreements with the Soviet Union while Gorbachev was at the height of his power.

Stalinization was the glue that held together the East European regimes. It was a code word for simply keeping the status quo in power. There was very little change, ever, for ordinary people; what change occurred was for the elite who had already accommodated themselves to the past and when the 1989 events unfolded they fit in with the new governments. Ordinary people could then travel and buy things after 1989 but they had no money. In the case of Poland the situation changed from one where the people faced empty shelves in stores to one where the people had empty pockets. Everyone celebrated what happened in 1989, the end of the Cold War, without asking what kind of capitalism would be suitable for Eastern Europe.

Lest we forget, the bipolar system was balanced during the Cold War. Soviet power was contained. But American power regarding Europe was also contained even as a number of pre-existing tendencies in American political culture were perpetuated and intensified.[7] Three times in American history the US resorted to conscription for war—and massive demobilization afterwards. These were the Civil War, World War I, and World War II. Only with the Cold War has the notion of ongoing readiness for war become a permanent part of the American system.[8] At the same time old cultural and historical roots of paranoia helped anti-communist hysteria become part of American political culture.[9]

## Europe and America Look at Each Other

American hegemony in the post World War II world has at times been a humiliating experience for Europe. The victory of the West in the Cold War, not unlike the victory of American military power in World War II, was a result that is itself bittersweet. There is a dichotomy in European attitudes on this point: they decry American domination yet they fear abandonment. Washington views Europe as lacking consistency and coherence, as not having the courage to come to terms with the complexity of their history. Yet how could it be otherwise as "Europe" is not a single entity such as the United States; Europe does not have a single telephone number, to paraphrase Kissinger. The "inconsistencies" which Americans see in European policies are the result of a fragmented history, a heritage of extreme differences.[10] In contrast, the US has had many historical luxuries and one of them has been a long coherent development with few of the disruptions which have beset Europe.

For these and other reasons the view from America is that the European continent looks more complicated than compelling. The European Union (EU), for example, is sufficiently split, sufficiently stable, and sufficiently stalled for back-burner status. For their part, Europeans find it difficult to accept the culture of American democracy, at times rejecting the American version. In Europe, democracy was born from a fear of the people; democratic advances were often a result of real or threatened violent popular movements.[11]

One of the great differences between Europe and the US today is that Europeans are involved in making nearly daily compromises to fit together in the European Union (EU). There is nothing very "grand" about this. It is the process of making a regional bloc of developed consumers. Americans, on the other hand, make periodic, not daily, choices about how to adjust to a worldly imperial role; it interferes little with daily life. There are few compromises to be made, nothing multicultural or multilingual about it. This transformation of the US into a global imperial power does not require the huge amount of paper just for translations that the EU does.

Animosity between Europe and the US is due in part to these divergent roles, notwithstanding the "good faith" of Obama and the favorable view of him abroad. The Europeans could play a greater role with the Americans, helping them to legitimize their "imperial" role by convincing Washington to downsize commitments. But few Americans are aware of this need and Europeans either don't have a clue as to why they are needed or, if they do get it, are unwilling to help. Could it be argued that the time would be ripe for a "Grand Communicator", a leader in Europe who can inspire and help argue for such a role? If so, the time would also be ripe in the US for a "Grand Design", with which to woo Europe as a partner not of necessity but of strategic choice. At stake are the hearts and minds of the people on both sides of the Atlantic.[12]

A fundamental problem increasingly shared by the governed in both the US and Europe is the issue of trust.[13] It was once thought that Italians had a monopoly on distrusting public officials. Worsening economic times have brought a level of populist distrust of those who govern on both sides of the Atlantic.[14] Alexis de Tocqueville observed long ago that the US was teeming with church groups, charities, clubs, associations that are good for society and that thrive between the realm of state and family, inculcating habits of helping democracy and capitalism. Society benefits to the extent that it has groups capable of generating "social capital" outside the circle of families. But as the population of developed societies continues to age and unemployment levels increase, the question is what kind of associational relationships beyond the family but below the state can produce trust.[15]

*Cold War Taboos and Europe: The Case of Italy*

The post-World War II world was the Cold War world. Within this context the Italian Communist Party (PCI) consistently developed and grew in strength to become the most powerful non-ruling communist party in the world. It was the only communist party of any significance anywhere that continued over time to revise its policies and strategy during the Cold War. In that way it kept up its level of electoral strength and, as the second largest political force in the country, grew in status as a major player in Italian politics. If the Cold War ended in 1989, the fall of the Berlin Wall was first felt in Italy only with the elections of 1994. Between 1989 and 1994 the PCI underwent a process of even greater change within a political system where many powerful Cold War parties completely disappeared, witness the fate of the largest party, the Christian Democrats (DC).[16]

In this disarray the Forza Italia movement was born and Silvio Berlusconi, a successful businessman from Milan, became a politician and winner of the 1994 elections. This date, 1994, signified the real end of the Cold War in Italy because it ended the isolation of the Far Right. There were two unbreakable rules during the Cold War in Italy. The communists should never come to power; the neo-Fascists should remain isolated. The 1994 elections saw the breakup of one of these taboos by bringing the Far Right party, the National Alliance (AN), into the ring of legitimacy. The other taboo regarding the communists in government ended shortly thereafter as the Democratic Party (PDS), representing most remnants of the old PCI, participated in succeeding government coalitions, beginning with the government headed by Romano Prodi.[17]

The big issue for Italy has been Europe. Italy is a founding nation of the EU, one of the original 6, and it is important for the Italians to remain a front line EU country. It is an issue of identity within the context of Europe. How can a country convince its citizens to endure sacrifices and reforms? Only by appealing to a higher order and that order in Italy is the EU. For the past several years Italians have been in the process of being "Europeanized." No other people in Europe are more pro-Europe and at the same time less enthusiastic about their own state.

Italians are among the longest living citizens in Europe and they also have one of the lowest fertility rates in the developed world. Over time, Italians risk becoming an endangered species.[18] A rising life expectancy is bitter sweet news in that an aging population raises the demand for pensions and health care as the number of working people needed to produce the necessary wealth to pay for these social obligations is declining.

The issues facing Italians are similar to the ones Germans faced last year and the French will face next year in their presidential elections.These issues have a lot to do with identity, both national and European. It is noteworthy that the more Islamic fundamentalists forcefully assert who they are in Europe, the more Europeans shrink from responding to the same question. Indeed the question of national versus European identity is never even asked. And it is neatly avoided in France by suggesting to Muslim women how they may dress in public.

*Security and Europe*

The Cold War has changed NATO's assumptions and its mission. Today NATO is likely to be asked to respond to threats of an extra-European nature, e.g., witness the war in Afghanistan. As an alliance NATO has advantages in being flexible: there is a good fit between historical legitimacy and the habit of allied countries accustomed to working together. A growing problem within NATO may be an inability to find consensus on defense issues when events unfold rapidly and when all member states don't feel the same sense of threat.[19] There is likely to be continued questioning between the US and NATO partners over what the alliance can and should do. NATO may become a "Coalition of the Unwilling."[20]

Among the concerns of NATO watchers there is likely to be what might be called the "revenge of history". This has nothing to do with the Cold War but it does have a lot to do with European regional history and the inter-war years before 1939. Future reform efforts must grasp the patterns of past conflicts in Europe. For example, NATO works and the United Nations doesn't and this might be called the lessons of Bosnia and Kosovo.

Yet the NATO story must play out in the overall framework of European relations with the US. And at no time in recent memory has Europe caught so little of America's attention than today. Paradoxically both Europe and the US want the US to be in NATO and lead NATO. Certainly the EU has a greater architecture today than it had in 1989; certainly today most of Europe has a good relationship with Russia. But does NATO have new tasks to perform? It seems basically to be about Afghanistan, the country that is the "graveyard of empires". In this light Afghanistan may prove to be decisive and be the conflict that sees NATO retain its form but lose its substance, lose its ability to act effectively.

Given the stress from severe economic problems facing the US the cost of placing American troops abroad is becoming an issue. Can the US afford its empire? This question is openly posed, even in conservative circles. Would a rough break, a sudden dismantling of American power abroad, be possible, perhaps culminating in a Vietnam-like exodus from Afghanistan? Since the Afghanistan intervention is a NATO intervention, would it not be better for the security of both the US and Europe to begin a smart downsizing and demilitarization of American policy, a controlled devolutionary trend?[21]

*The Obama Administration: Back to the Future?*

Americans tend to be operational liberals and philosophical conservatives. When considering American politics one is reminded of Mark Twain's comment

about Wagner's music: "its better than it sounds." Yet money is increasingly becoming the coin of American politics and therefore many voices will not be
heard. Samuel Butler's remark that "a hen is only an egg's way of making another egg" comes to mind when considering what has happened to American political parties. A modern, trans-Atlantic application of Butler's remark could be
that political parties can be seen as machines made by politicians for the purpose
of making copies of themselves.

Before Obama JFK was the last American president who was unapologetic
about being smart. Clinton had a fake folksy manner about him and Bush
adopted anti-intellectualism as a policy. To date Obama has had a few milestones: the financial reforms, health care reform, the speech in Cairo; these have
helped change positively the image of the United States around the world.

Considerable media attention has been focused on Obama's "great openings",
to Cuba, to Iran, and to the Islamic world in general through his Cairo speech.
Yet Obama has basically continued the Bush administration's policy towards
Russia. While Obama's desire is to reset relations with Europe as with Russia the
problem in the latter case is that the last thing the Russians want is to reset relations with the United States. The Russians do not want to go back to the period
after the collapse of the Soviet Union which they regard as an economic and
geopolitical disaster. The Obama administration essentially considers that the
Russians have no legitimate right to claim priority in the former Soviet Union
while the United States has the right to develop bilateral relations with any country and expand NATO as it wishes. The Americans have viewed the Russian leadership as unwilling to follow the basic architecture of relations that had developed after 1991 and as being unreasonable in redefining what the Americans
thought was a stable and desirable relationship.[22]

Obama has adopted the Bush administration's policy of a phased withdrawal
from Iraq keyed to a process of political stabilization. But he has increased the
number of US troops committed to Afghanistan and shifted from a purely defensive one to a mixed posture of selective offense and defense. Even so, his basic
strategy remains the same as Bush's: hold in Afghanistan until the political situation evolves to the point that a political settlement is possible. So the little thorn
in the side of Obama's foreign policy is the evolving war in Afghanistan, a war
that looks more like Vietnam every day. Obama argues, as did Bush before him,
that the war is driven by necessity. This is the one area that disappoints those
seeking in Obama a transformational American president.

1. See Chapter 1 in Andrew J. Bacevich, *The Limits of Power* (New York: Metropolitan Books, 2008); Chapters 1 and 2 in H.W. Brands, *American Dreams* (New York: Penguin, 2010).

2. See the interview with Vice President Joe Biden, "Biden Says Weakened Russia Will Bend to Us", *Wall Street Journal*, July 25, 2009.

3. Chapter 1 in Steven W. Hook and John Spanier, *American Foreign Policy Since World War II,* (Washington D.C.:CQ Press, 2007); Part 11 in Randall B. Woods and Howard Jones, *Dawning of the Cold War* (Chicago: Ivan Dee, 1991).

4. For a discussion of the isolationist impulse see Michael D. Pearlman, *Warmaking and American Diplomacy* (Lawrence: University Press of Kansas, 1999); for a discussion of the history of the interventionist side of US foreign policy see Emily S. Rosenberg, *Spreading the American Dream* (New York: Hill and Wang, 1982).

5. Chapter 3 in Christopher Layne, *The Peace of Illusions* (Ithaca: Cornell University Press, 2006); Chapters 1-3 in Melvyn P. Leffler, *A Preponderance of Power* (Stanford: Stanford University Press, 1992).

6. Part 4 in Christian G. Appy, ed., *Cold War Constructions* (Amherst: University of Massachusetts Press, 2000); Introduction in Anatol Lieven, *America Right or Wrong*, (Oxford: Oxford University Press, 2004).

7. See Introduction in David Calleo, *Follies of Power: America's Unipolar Fantasy* (Cambridge: Cambridge University Press, 2009).

8. Introduction in Martin McCauley, *Russia, America and the Cold War* (London: Pearson, 2004); also Martin McCauley, *The Origins of the Cold War 1941-1940* (London: Pearson, 2003).

9. In the nineteenth century there was a fear among American Protestants that a Catholic army could invade the United States by balloons. Such levels of fantasy can be seen in the cinema as well, for example, the popular film "Red Dawn", when Soviet and Nicaraguan troops succeed in winning a world war and occupy the United States. On Cold War propaganda see Introduction in Walter L. Hixson, *Parting the Curtain* (New York: St. Martin's Griffin, 1998); Chapter 1 in Andrew D. Grossman, *Neither Dead Nor Red* (New York: Routledge, 2001).

10. Chapters 1 and 2 in Lieven, *America Right or Wrong*.

11.Chapters 1 and 7 in John Lewis Gaddis, *The Cold War* (New York: Penguin, 2005).

12. Chapter 2 in Lieven, *America Right or Wrong*.

13. Part 2 and 3 in Francis Fukuyama, *Trust* (New York:Free Press, 1995)

14. A discussion of the "dreams" of European and American government and how people at a populist level react can be found in Jeremy Rifkin, *The European Dream*, (New York: Penguin, 2004).

15. Part 4 in Tony Judt, *Postwar* (London: Penguin, 2006).

16. See the discussion in Vassilis Fouskas, *Italy, Europe, The Left* (Aldershot: Ashgate, 1998).

17. Part 2 in Robert Leonardi and Raffaella Y. Nanetti, eds., *Italy: Politics and Policy*, Volume 1 (Aldershot: Dartmouth, 1996).

18. Chapter 15 in Ariane Chebel d'Appollonia and Simon Reich, *Immigration, Integration, and Security* (Pittsburgh: University of Pittsburgh Press, 2008).

19. Chapters 19 and 20 in Walter LaFeber, *The American Age* (New York: Norton, 1994)

20. See Conclusion in John Lamberton Harper, *American Visions of Europe* (Cambridge: Cambridge University Press, 1996)

21. See the Ron Paul interview in *Time magazine* September 18, 2009; an alternative to American hegemony is discussed in Chapter 6, T.R. Reid, *The United States of Europe* (New York: Penguin, 2004).

22. Chapter 5 in Lieven, *America Right or Wrong*; Chapter 5 in Layne, *The Peace of Illusions*.

*Gian Paolo Calchi Novati*

# The Defeat of the Third World: The Case of the Horn of Africa

The Third World was an important theatre of the Cold War.[1] The East-West confrontation mainly took place in Europe, notably Berlin, divided by the Iron Curtain that Churchill dramatically denounced in 1946 from Missouri.[2] In Europe the borders had been sketched at Yalta, and to some extent they were mutually accepted as stable. In the Third World, whose members got independence country by country as a consequence of the process of decolonization after the Second World War, all situations were in flux. The former colonial territories were the theatre where "free world" and "international communism" did compete and even waged war without the danger of stirring up the nuclear holocaust. The newly independent nations of Africa, Asia and the Middle East were in principle neither capitalist nor socialist and were looking for progress, aid, and protection. The counterweights typical of the bipolar order allowed them to approach either bloc and even to shift from one bloc to another. The relationships of the Periphery with the powers of the Center were by definition asymmetric, but the South had the chance to profit from this East-West rivalry. Therefore, the end of the bipolar system deprived the Third World of some opportunities.

Africa didn't escape the burdens of the Cold War and yet no multilateral military pact comparable to NATO, SEATO or the Baghdad Pact was exported to the Black Continent. The United States respected the jurisdiction of the European powers. Security, i. e. freedom of access to natural and strategic resources, was entrusted to the former colonial powers, namely Britain and France, who were the major allies of the United States in the global system. Only where the colonial powers were weakest did the United States pursue a more direct role in Africa as well. American interventions in the Congo and Angola replaced Belgium and Portugal in dealing with the turmoil in the aftermath of independence. It was above all the case of the Horn, where the main colonial power had been Italy, a middle-sized power with a weak status in the international order. The

Horn of Africa—the area that encompasses the present-day states of Ethiopia, Somalia, Eritrea and Djibouti, plus Sudan, which is the link between the proper Horn and the Nile Valley—has been the victim of frequent clashes between the superpowers through the entire period of the Cold War. However the initiative was definitely in the hands of the local actors.

Historically, Ethiopia has been the core of the Horn.[3] Together with Liberia, Ethiopia was the only African state which, apart from the five-year parenthesis of Italian occupation after the invasion of 1935, preserved its independence from colonialism. The state of Somalia emerged in 1960 as a potential challenger to Ethiopia in the regional geostrategic scheme of things. Mogadishu advocated the unification of all the lands inhabited by Somali-speaking people. In order to match Ethiopia, which had a special relationship with the United States and had signed a formal alliance in 1953 by way of a partly classified treaty, Somalia sought the support of the USSR from the very beginning of its tormented history as an independent state. In fact, nobody in the West was eager to sponsor a nation that defied the post-colonial *status quo* in Africa with irredentism and revisionism. Italy, the former colonial power, refused to provide weapons to Mogadishu failing to abide by her supposed duty as a former colonial power. Pan-Somalism meant putting into question the borders and territory of three or four states in the region starting from the Ethiopian province of Ogaden.

In 1970, one year after the army's *coup d'état*, the Government of Somalia adopted 'scientific socialism' as its official doctrine. It was the first African state which proclaimed the intention to push the socialist option beyond the gambit of the 'African socialism' preached by Nkrumah and Sékou Touré, Senghor, and Nyerere. Thus, Mogadishu's relation with Moscow was consequently revised under the new circumstances. Nevertheless, a basic misunderstanding continued to undermine the partnership. Breaking up established states was not in line with the current praxis. When Siyad Barre needed support on the battlefield, Moscow maintained that its obligations did not cover Pan-Somalism and Brezhnev stepped back from the Somali invasion of Ethiopian territory.

The overall crisis of Africa during the 1970s and the 1980s revealed that the Black Continent lacked the requisites to fully enjoy the rewards of interdependence that other developing countries had been able to grasp.[4] Italian colonialism was cancelled by a decision made by international diplomacy, as a result of the Italian defeat in World War II rather than along a proper decolonization process with a confrontation between the colonized and the colonizers in view of an agreed transfer of power from metropolitan rule to African representatives.[5] On the whole the former Italian possessions in the Horn were more vulnerable than other African countries to the winds of the uneasy transition to democracy and development.

They suffered because of their isolation from financial inputs and technological innovations. Hence, they were plagued with chronic instability and diffuse belligerence.[6] Italian patronage was not a credible shield. Neo-colonialism is a demanding assignment for it implies the will and tools to exercise influence over client states in the Periphery forsaking outright control of the territory. The dismal reality is that Italy did not succeed in establishing the practice of mutual collaboration and complicity that had been the normal outlet of European imperialism and had often proved to be more resilient to direct administration. As the Eritrean scholar Uoldelul Chelati says, "a major regional colonial power [...] evaporated already by 1941 and failed in fulfilling its historical 'mission' of bridging colonized societies to decolonization and achieving either through negotiation or conflict the empowerment of local elites in the post-colonial state."[7]

As stated by the parameters of decolonization in Africa,[8] reaffirmed by the Organization of African Union (OAU) in its very first resolution once founded in Addis Ababa in 1963, any independent state corresponded to a former colonial territory. The pseudo-decolonization that took place in the Horn didn't abide by such a dogma.[9] The two former Italian colonies either lost or changed their own colonial outline; Eritrea, the *colonia primogenita*, was annexed to Ethiopia and Italian Somalia merged with British Somaliland into the new Republic of Somalia with Mogadishu as the capital.

Italy tried to make up for her operative limits as a "half-power" by multiplying initiatives and courting an assortment of partners at the same time. This strategy led to a number of contradictory aims—Somalia *versus* Ethiopia, self-determination *versus* established state integrity, sympathy for liberation fronts *versus* cooperation with legal or *de facto* governments—that in the end it was unable to reconcile.[10]

Given the sharp polarization of the Italian domestic political system, heavily conditioned by the international alignments of its main political parties, it was simply not feasible to devise any bipartisan policy in the Horn. The result has been a sort of "partisan bi-policy". The policy was partisan; sometimes it was conducted differently by different parties belonging to the same coalition, and even by different factions (*correnti*) of each single party, never mind whether they were in government or in opposition. This odd predicament prevented a consistent and affirmative approach to the rights of African nations and a regional equilibrium. Within the binding rules of the East-West confrontation, Italy's presence in the Third World was quite palatable to nationalist forces in Africa. Nationalism in Africa and in the Arab countries had little or nothing to fear from an ex-colonial power deprived of its possessions and without neo-imperial ambitions. Indeed, weakness was a meek but momentous asset, since it helped Italy to act without raising the mistrust of the interlocutors. The irony was that the decline of the West in a Third World nation—as it occurred in the Horn with Somalia's leaning toward the Soviet Union up to the drafting of a Treaty of Friendship and Co-operation in 1974 or with the military assistance granted to Ethiopia by the USSR in 1977—was likely to boost rather than emasculate Italian political self-promotion as a last resort for a Western presence. Sliding into the "socialist" camp did not jeopardize, as such, Italian action in the Horn.

Geography determines politics more than anything else in the ancient and recent history of the Horn of Africa. The balance of power in the region that comprises the modern states of Ethiopia, Eritrea, Somalia and Djibouti—plus Sudan, the link between the proper Horn and the Nile Valley—shows a complex multifaceted picture with a number of inter-linkages. The Horn has suffered from tensions and permanent instability due to the unresolved conflicts between the groups that—for reasons of nationality, linguistic and cultural affiliation, social status, etc.—hold dominant positions and the groups that, for the same reasons but with inverse results, are or feel excluded, exploited or marginalized. Imperial control has intermittently been challenged by local resistance and opposition movements, committed in their own way to create kingdoms and identities suitable to the characteristics and expectations of the subordinated groups. In our case-study, the "center-periphery" scheme can be verified at three levels: domestic cleavages, regional rivalry, and the level of international tensions.

A first level of contrast involves those powers which have demonstrated their ability to control the human and physical pattern and, on the other side, the socio-political structures that did not have full access to sovereignty and resources. Ancient empires were replaced by modern states that, in turn, used their might to the detriment of "non-historical" nations with neither territory nor sovereignty. The past myths were revived so as to keep internal unity and hegemony in the surrounding areas. The populations which have been, over time, absorbed through cooptation and coercion are treated like a sort of "periphery" within the states. The movements of resistance and opposition to the most influential powers brought about dynamics in pursuit of administrations and identities more suitable to the characteristics and expectations of the subordinated groups. The wars, both intra and inter-state, were in essence a continuation of politics by other means. The texture of internal relations, based more on hostility than cooperation, has endured throughout the Horn's history. It remained more or less intact even when the Horn fell under the rule or the threat of outside forces during the colonial era and in the years of the Cold War. The Horn proved to be one of the most troublesome battlegrounds in the struggle between East and West to control the Third World.

The second dimension of unrest in the Horn regards conflicts at the regional level. The populations and states in the Horn compete against each other more than they confront foreign powers. The stakes at the heart of this conflict include land, water, ports and economic resources, but also non-material goods such as sovereignty, the institutional pattern, and hegemony. Traditions of statehood differ greatly from country to country and ruling governments fear that the presence of rival models could imperil their very existence.[11]

The third level of tension or belligerence refers to the repercussions of great policy and the transposition of international conflicts into the Horn. In this context, the *Scramble for Africa* played a special role, engaging half a dozen European powers in the second half of the XIX century. The colonial period in the Horn—1869 to 1941—marked the peak of outright interference by external powers, eager to seize local resources and strategic assets. In spite of all the characteristics of a foreign intrusion, colonialism differed in the fact that it exercised a direct jurisdiction overseas from within. The main colonial powers in the Horn were Italy and Britain. France established its own possession—the Somali Coast around the port-city of Djibouti—and broadly challenged the exclusive influence of Italy and Britain without competing for confining territories.

With the advent of colonialism, a minority of a different cultural and religious origin forcefully established itself in the Horn, tampering with the already existing territorial and national assets. The metropolitan "center" exploits labor in the form of *corvées,* serfdom or slavery, and takes control of natural resources for further capitalist development. Italy sought to occupy the land in order to establish settlers, while the principal objective of England was control of water: the Nile basin and the routes to India through the Suez Canal, the Red Sea and the Indian Ocean. The previous system of domination and subordination between states and between the various groups within them was definitively altered. By way of institutional and productive transformation, colonialism redesigned the political, economic and cultural environment. Colonialism was perceived and accepted in different ways by various groups along their position in the power ladder, ranging from resistance to complicity and collaboration. European nations exploited local contrasts in order to accomplish their plans. For this reason they supported those elements which might have facilitated their expansion and power by promising the marginalized peoples to subvert their status of subjugation.

Colonialism did not destroy the pre-existing ideologies, but, imposing a technologically and politically superior authority on previously unknown cultural and institutional paradigms, it severely altered internal dynamics. The outcomes of the colonial predicament were shaped by factors such as time, density, political designs, and the presence of settlers. Italian colonialism was labeled "demographic colonialism", but, after all, settlers in the Horn were a tiny minority with respect to the local population. The case of Libya was quite different.

The colonial interlude was decisive in the formation of states and nations. The form of administration introduced by the European powers displaced or transformed the local order. The colonial management of land and resources was more efficient but aggravated and intensified the chronic instability due to protest against the occupation, loss of sovereignty, and the expropriation of goods. Sometimes the resistance escalated into an all-out war. Colonialism as such, without meaningful distinction from one power to another, stressed the importance of ethnicity since in a situation where a foreign culture is imposed, coupled with political dominance and expropriation of resources, clan and familial allegiances are the most immediate means of survival. While the curbed and harassed rulers defend, on principle, their power and national liberty, colonialism can help the losers of the past to surpass their position of inferiority. Indeed, subordinated groups are driven to ease the penetration of colonialism in hopes of getting rid of their old masters. The colonial experience leaves a lasting legacy either by separating subject peoples from the ruling centers and thus liberating them from traditional obligations or by confirming pre-existing relations of domination.

Ethiopia and Sudan bravely counteracted colonial imperialism thanks to their political and military might. The reformers who governed Ethiopia in the second half of the XIX century (the emperors Tewodros and Menelik) and the Mahdist state in Sudan achieved their own designs for the centralization of power in the fissures left by the colonial partition of Africa carried out by the European powers. Italy mobilized the subjugated peoples against Ethiopia, who suffered expansion and occupation, and in some way legitimized the separateness of Eritrea and the would-be requests of the Somalis. Similarly, in Sudan, British occupation complicated the relationship between the Southern Black peoples and the Arab-Muslim power rooted in the North. Also in the ensuing periods, Ethiopia and Sudan staunchly stood up for the *status quo* and by contrast Eritrea and Somalia—Eritrea for a long time as a liberation movement, Somalia as an example of Pan-Somali ideology—embraced revisionist policies.

Outside influence was also manifested by an interaction of local actors and powers and superpowers that, in contrast to the colonial powers, did not seek direct control or sovereignty in the Horn. Such was the case for the Arab states—commencing with Sudan, the closest Arab state to the Horn. And such was the case for the superpowers during the Cold War. The peculiarity was that the Horn's nations succeeded in exploiting the East-West confrontation to prop up their own national causes—Ethiopia defended the integrity of the state with the help of the United States,[12] Somalia relied on the Soviet Union in order to recover the Somali lands claimed by Mogadishu—rather than deliver their territories and resources to the service of global players.

In the aftermath of the revolution which ousted the monarchy and abolished feudalism in Ethiopia, Somalia made use of the vacuum to implement the long-standing Pan-Somali dream and invaded the Ethiopian territory—nom-inally, to back the Somali-speaking tribes in Ogaden and the struggle of the Western Somalia Liberation Front. The military treaty that linked USA and Ethiopia had not yet been repudiated but Washington kept Ethiopia at a distance because of the radical course inaugurated by the military regime. Somali President Mohammed Siyad Barre hurried back to Moscow to press the Kremlin to deliver the assistance apparently promised by the Friendship and Cooperation Treaty of 1974. Brezhnev—on vacation at a Black Sea resort—did not even receive him, rebuffing his hopes. The sanctity of the borders was an established principle in the bipolar order. The US and the USSR wholly agreed to prevent conquests and secessions.

Ethiopia was put on the American "black list" of countries responsible for human rights violations. The military base of Kagnew Station was no longer essential to US strategy as it had been in the past. That base had been for many years the main consequence of good relations between the United States and Ethiopia. It was a pillar in the American system of international communications thanks to the altitude and the latitude of Asmara. In the 1970s it became obsolete because of the development of satellite intelligence and the creation of the huge base of Diego Garcia in the Indian Ocean. So, the US was ready to leave Ethiopia to its own destiny. Mengistu Haile Mariam, the Red Negus, who had won a bloody feud at the top of the Derg (Council or Committee in amharic, as the military junta was commonly called), did not hesitate to solicit military aid from the USSR in order to replace the weapons which came from the West. The Soviet advisors moved from Mogadishu to Addis Ababa. A process of de-alignment and re-alignment took place in the space of a few months. Somalia was strongly encouraged to attack Ethiopia by some sort of an *ante litteram* Islamic "camp", then composed of the Shah's Iran, Saudi Arabia, and Egypt, who wanted to chase the "communists" out of the Horn. The local actors had proven once more capable of maintaining firmly the initiative in their hands. For Somalia, the result of the maneuver was disappointing. The US limited its military support to the withdrawal of the last soldier of the Somali army from Ethiopian territory. Siyad Barre had lost his major partner without a prompt and totally satisfactory replacement.[13]

By the end of the Cold War, the Soviet Union—and, later, Russia—completely moved out of the African theatre. The new Russian leadership reckoned their disproportionate exposure in Angola and in the Horn was a major cause of the collapse of the Soviet Union and Socialism. Zbignew Brzezinski, the advisor to President Carter for National Security, summed up a predominant view by saying that "détente is buried in the sands of Ogaden." Perhaps this assumption was an exaggeration. Nevertheless, the Russian-Cuban intervention in Ethiopia with troops, heavy weapons and large-scale military assistance was the second big effort brought about in Africa by Brezhnev after the intervention in Angola in 1975. Perhaps such a challenge was too much for US susceptibility. In 1960, the radical experiment attempted by Patrice Lumumba after the independence of Belgian Congo hoping to rely on Soviet sponsorship was badly wrecked and Lumumba himself was assassinated by his enemies. The Soviet Union demonstrated its powerlessness as it still lacked the machinery that was needed for long distance military operations. The fact that fifteen years later the Soviet Union successfully supported Agostinho Neto in halting the offensive of Zaire and the South African expeditionary force revealed that the balance of power in the former colonial world had undergone a profound transformation.

The entire scenario in the Horn abruptly changed in 1991 following a political earthquake with three main effects: (a) the breakdown and dismemberment of Somalia since the warlords who fought a civil war against Siyad Barre once his regime was overthrown kept firm and exclusive control of their respective tribal areas instead of building up a national government; (b) the full independence of Eritrea under the leadership of the Eritrean People's Liberation Front (EPLF) engaged in a 30-year war of liberation/secession from Ethiopia; (c) the introduction in Ethiopia by the post-Derg regime—a coalition of parties dominated by the Tigray People's Liberation Front (TPLF)— of a form of federalism and decentralization on a regional and ethnic basis. Ethiopia's new Constitution opens with the striking words "We, the Nations, Nationalities and Peoples of Ethiopia" and provides for the right to self-determination up to secession of the various groups. The military triumph of both EPLF and TPLF was facilitated by an adjustment of their alliances abjuring Marxism-Leninism and calling on the West's benevolence. Israel as well endorsed the birth of the Eritrean independent nation once it was clear that the former Italian colony would not become an Arab or Islamic state.

Italy could be proud of a posthumous and unexpected success, in a sense. Fifty years or so after losing her possessions in the Horn, the mark of colonialism re-emerged in force, overcoming the Great Tradition of the Empire and Pan-Somalism. In fact, the division of Somalia into two different states according to colonial boundaries, and the secession of Eritrea from Ethiopia, reproduced the geopolitics of the Scramble. Colonialism strikingly confirmed its function as an unbeatable "state maker"[14]

Nevertheless, Italian policy in the Horn had always privileged "statehood". But the state shattered against the hard realities of civil wars. Oddly, those who gained were the two movements-parties, the EPLF in Eritrea and the TPLF in Ethiopia, the two that Italy's policy had neglected the most. The flight of Siyad Barre from Mogadishu in January 1991 was the last act of a regime that Italy had tirelessly tried to preserve for over twenty years as a token of stability. Italy's influence did not recover from these blows. The Somali National University—the jewel of Italian technical assistance—was destroyed and vandalized during the onslaught of the militias. Italy supplied political and economic aid to Siyad Barre besieged in Villa Somalia as long as possible. Aghast and bitter, a number of Italian expatriates watched as passive bystanders the final battle for control of the capital city of the former colony. The Italian embassy in Mogadishu was the last one to be evacuated—a sign of responsibility, perhaps, and a strong demonstration of Italy's will to stay on, but at the same time, above all in the perception of Siyad Barre's enemies, the proof of a special relationship with the dying regime.

Due to a long state tradition, Ethiopia was supposed to be very different from Somalia, a *parvenu* in the family of states in the Horn. In fact, in 1991, Addis Ababa fell, under circumstances roughly equivalent to Mogadishu, but with less bloodshed and without such a rout of the central authority. To the dismay of Italian efforts deployed in order to remain close to any government in Addis Ababa, the United States and not Italy played a leading role in the last days of the fighting that caused the end of Mengistu's regime and the flight abroad of the Red Negus. The new Government sanctioned the independence of Eritrea giving up the embattled province and access to the sea—a historical post for any Ethiopian government. The two liberation movements ganged up against the Derg. The independence of Eritrea, which crowned a long and controversial struggle,[15] was unanimously approved both by the United Nations and the Organization of African Union. At least in the Horn, the inviolability of the colonial and de-colonial boundaries was put aside—though Eritrea was a very special case since it had been a colonial territory separated from Ethiopia up to World War II.[16]

In the so-called New World Order proclaimed by President George H.W. Bush in 1990, the Horn was affected by external tensions ions even more sternly than in Cold War times.[17] Africa was singled out by Bush as a main issue of US foreign policy after the end of the Communist threat because of its immense reservoir of energy, minerals, and strategic assets, all of them indispensable for further development and security of the US and its allies.[18] The Horn has been the sole African theatre of a major military intervention without the protection that had been ensured by East-West dualism. Somalia proved sensitive to the contagion of the instability that characterized the international system in the new situation and quietly became a target of the war on terror declared by George W. Bush after the Twin Towers catastrophe. The Ethiopian Government led by Meles Zenawi was ready to play the Big Game siding American pre-emptive action against any symptom of Islamic upsurge in Somalia. The Horn has always been perceived by the superpowers, especially by the United States, as an appendix of the Middle East. In February 1945, President Roosevelt, returning from Yalta, received Emperor Haile Selassie in Egypt and on the same occasion he met the King of Egypt and the King of Saudi Arabia stressing the connection between Ethiopia, with her Christian court, and the Arab world.[19] Thus, in the post-bipolar order the Horn has been charged with the same questions that afflict the Middle East, i. e. the security of Israel, oil, Islam. Israel, in fact, has played a primary role in the Horn and in Sudan, sustaining and arming anti-Arab and anti-Muslim forces.

While Somalia was ravaged by civil war, in a crescendo of anarchy and famine, the US—and, later, the UN—carried out the operation that was unwisely named "Restore Hope". The interdictions of the Cold War balance were over. For the first time, former colonial powers and superpowers had the chance to undertake a direct intervention in Africa against the will of the host country. Italy had the advantage of being acquainted with the terrain better than other nations and was invited, like Britain, to dispatch troops.

Strictly speaking, Somalia does not fit the region that has hosted the major wars after the end of bipolarism. Yet Somalia had a common fate with the Greater Middle East, the Balkans, and Central Asia. In a US Senate hearing in 1999, General Normam Schwartzkopf explained why the area that contains the Suez Canal in the North and the Bab-el-Mandeb in the South was so crucial for the West's defense plans. In a column contributed to the *Washington Post* in the post-Twin Towers political climate, Susan Rice—former Assistant Secretary of State for African Affairs who later was appointed by Obama as the US ambassador to the United Nations—wrote: "If America has to win, and not just to fight, the war on terror, it cannot consider Africa as separated from the comprehensive global war."

The objectives of the ill-conceived and poorly executed "Restore Hope" Operation, launched by Bush in December 1992, were confused and not stated in advance. The United Nations joined the operation in 1993 taking the lead. Italy sent troops keeping an autonomous line of conduct.[20] The Italian command frequently clashed with the destructive policy of the US contingent, which focused on Mohammed Farah Aidid, the troublesome warlord that the American Government, for a while, addressed as its main enemy. The battle in October 1993, in which 18 American rangers and hundreds, perhaps thousands, of Somalis died, during a raid of the American troops in order to catch or kill Aidid, made an enormous impression in America, and compelled the United States to shut down "Restore Hope." The episode was illustrated by Ridley Scott's movie *Black Hawk Down*. Only a few months later Aidid was rehabilitated by the American authorities and amicably traveled with the US special envoy on an American aircraft to Addis Ababa for talks with his Somali counterparts. The international force was withdrawn by March 1995, ostensibly without any positive outcome. The peak of the famine was over but Somalia was in pieces and the climate of anarchy was even worse than before.

The dismal experience in Somalia suggested to some generals of the Pentagon the necessity of a comprehensive reassessment of the agenda of military multilateral operations. No more interventions abroad under the aegis of a foreign command—included the United Nations. No more operations without acknowledgeable and predefined aims. No more nation-building missions in backward and divided countries.[21]

After 9/11 President George Bush scrutinized Somalia for possible collusion with Al-Qaeda and the terrorist network of fundamentalist Islam. Al-Ittihad, a religious group widely involved in charity activities all over the country, was accused of being a terrorist organization and Somalia was suspected of offering sanctuaries to Islamic terrorists. The assets of Barakat, a big banking and telecom company that managed most of the formal and informal business in Somalia and within the Somali diaspora in America and in the Gulf, were frozen, allegedly for hidden links to Al-Qaeda. On the eve of the strike against the regime in Kabul after the Twin Towers attack, the American press recommended that the "Somali lesson" not be forgotten. But to some extent the US embarked on the same path that had already been tried in Somalia. Indeed, Somalia was identified as a possible outlet for the surviving Taleban and Al-Qaeda forces fleeing Afghanistan. In fact, the political, religious and ecological pattern of Somalia is suggestive of Afghanistan's framework: territory mainly of shrubs and desert, a weak central government, sectarianism, illicit trade, and a booming expansion of political Islam. After 9/11 enforcing the law and controlling the territory was by far more important than providing flexible and easy access to investments and goods. The power void in Somalia would be no more tolerable to either the United States or Ethiopia.[22]

As in other comparable situations (i.e. the transition of Algeria from a one-party state to a multiparty system), violence became an integral part of the growth of Islamic fundamentalism. In Somalia, jihadism seemed a way to get rid of fragmentation, anarchy, and instability. Islamic Courts—which so far had managed local power and traditional law in the interstices of the warlords' jurisdiction—formed their own militia and in June 2006 took power in Mogadishu without any serious resistance. At first, Islamic appeal was very strong: rule and order, and charitable welfare for everybody. The re-unification assured by Muslim ideology was a good alternative to the split in struggling clans. The Muslim movement had the inspired idea of so-called "little solutions for big problems". That was enough for the Somali population after so many years of despair and bad governance. Also in Somalia, however, the "Kingdom of God"—the project of a policy capable of renovating human beings on behalf of a superior morality—was not on hand. After initial mass support, harsh measures and abuses in the name of rigid orthodoxy spread mixed feelings and discontent.

Ethiopia saw in the access to power of the Union of Islamic Courts the long-awaited justification to intensify its pressure on the borders of Somalia. It was essential for Meles to eradicate the menace represented by political Islam at the borders, not only as a possible drive to rebellion of the Somali majority in Ogaden but also as an incentive that might galvanize the Muslim community living in Ethiopia (more or less 50% of the entire population). Finally, at the end of 2006 Meles started on the military invasion and occupation, or semi-occupation, of Somalia, toppling the Islamic government and literally transporting a complacent President and his ministers to Mogadishu in Ethiopian tanks. From the start, the President of the Transitional Federal Government (TFG), Abdoulahi Yusuf, was considered pro-Ethiopian, and his appointment had been enthusiastically welcomed by Addis Ababa. Nobody supported Somalia. Yet more evidence that the post-bipolar system was intimately different from the bipolar one. For sure, the new order doesn't warrant the rights of a peripheral country under attack when the aggressor enjoys the favor of the United States. As a matter of fact, Ethiopia was backed, encouraged and condoned by Washington.

The initiative taken by Meles was another illustration of how in the Horn local actors redefine the meaning of international strategies in pursuit of national interests. However, whereas during the Cold War, the Horn's states were careful to uphold their reasons first and to take profit from the Soviet-American rivalry in order to accomplish them with the help of a superpower, Ethiopia tried to anticipate the wishes of the only superpower fighting her small "war on terror". Such a mix of national and global concerns proved to be a misstep. Ethiopia underestimated the hostility of the Somalis to any foreign interference and was drawn into a game beyond the range of her limited means. Nationalism, Islamic revivalism, and the local branch of Al-Qaeda coalesced against the TFG, installed and protected by the Ethiopian troops, giving way to the hardliners. Despite its original endorsement by international diplomacy (the Inter-Governmental Authority for Development (IGAD) had mediated the negotiations which brought about the setting up of the Transitional Federal Government in 2004), now most Somalis viewed the Government as just a stooge of Somalia's historical enemy.

Ethiopia envisaged two goals which were intrinsically contradictory: carving out a corridor through Somali territory to ensure access to the sea for her export-import trade by-passing the Eritrean ports, un-accessible after the Eritrea-Ethiopia war of 1998-2000, and preventing any threat of destabilization across the Somali borders. Meles had to choose between safety and expansionism. The latter—a direct or indirect control of parts of Somali territory—implies a Somalia with no central authority. But an impotent Somalia would be doomed to offer an easy 'haven' to terrorists; a supplementary nuisance derived from regional alignments. Ethiopia has always been put, conventionally, in the anti-Arab or anti-Muslim camp. Egypt—in its capacity of being a Muslim state—is, in a way, the guarantee of the independence of Somalia. Although Ethiopia is a valuable and appreciated ally, Egypt would be a priority in American strategy.

After a short but promising honeymoon,[23] local, regional, and international factors triggered in May 1998 another conflict in the Horn, between Eritrea and Ethiopia, nominally over a boundary controversy.[24] The *casus belli* was above all the locality of Badme, held by the Ethiopians and claimed by the Eritreans. Unlike most African wars, it was an "inter-state" war, not an "intra state" one. Italy felt some responsibility because the border had been traced when it was the colonial power both in Ethiopia and Eritrea.[25] Unluckily the records issued by the *Istituto Geografico Militare* in Florence were not decisive as the border differed from the one indicated in the maps.[26] The usual ambivalence of the Italian government not choosing clearly between the two belligerents and maintaining an equidistant position, thwarted its attempts to be an effective mediator.

The war, beyond the pretext of sovereignty over miles of stones and dry rivers, regarded resources (transit trade, use of ports, etc.) and such immaterial goods as supremacy at the regional and international level.[27] Post-independence revisionism in Asmara had destroyed the equilibrium all over the Horn in an essentially anti-Ethiopian rationale.[28] Revisionism is typical of diasporic nations.[29] We have already mentioned the case of Somalia. Eritrea also stood vigil over its controversial version of nationalism. In contrast, Ethiopia championed as always the *status quo* in terms of both territory and influence. To the great dismay of Meles, Eritrea placed its revisionism on the bandwagon of the Islamic movement in Somalia sheltering the most radical wing—an unholy alliance since the Government in Eritrea is strictly Christian and has, in turn, marginalized the pro-Muslim party.

Arguing from another perspective, the 1998 war was just one round in the competition between the two rivals to test their credibility and demonstrate who could or should better provide "praetorians" for US operations in the region that stretches from North Africa to the Indian Ocean. The juxtaposition between the adamant resistance to colonialism by the Ethiopians and the connivance with Italy's aggressions of the Eritreans through a mass enrollment in the colonial troops (*ascari*) in 1896 and in 1935, has been a permanent component of the political discourse in the Horn marking the chasm between the two peoples and the two countries.[30] In the post-bipolar system, in Africa as in the Periphery at large, even competitors and rivals are compelled to please the same possible allies at the international level. Eritrea has good reason to complain that the Ethiopian Government refused to implement the verdict pronounced by the international Commission charged to define the contested frontier.[31] The Commission gave satisfaction to Asmara just in the crucial area of Badme. Yet Isaias Afeworki recognizes that the Americans are the only ones who may persuade Meles to change his mind.

The structure of the international system is in perpetual evolution and American willpower alone doesn't suffice to resolve the imbalance. A multipolar world that would place many players on equal footing is still just rhetoric. Nonetheless, the concurrence of China could re-open the game, also in the Horn. The concurrency of China with the Western powers has been mainly confined to aid and investments. China prefers not to sharpen the clash with the US in view of a possible boosting of a G2 arrangement for governing the world.

In the current system the integrity of the African states is not protected like in the Cold War order of the past. In the Horn the territorial *status quo* has been already altered (Eritrea, Somaliland). The next challenge will be the future of Sudan, on the eve of a referendum with an exit option of the Southern provinces. The dismemberment of Sudan and even more of Congo, another country whose unity is at risk, could be a more dreadful precedent for the entire continent.

Starting from the Horn and the trans-Saharan region, Africa is going to be attracted more and more into the Arab world and thus into a post-Cold War global confrontation. Humanitarian aid dispensed by the Muslim Brotherhood can take the place of aid provided by those Western NGOs that are in retreat. Islamism represents an important factor of aggregation and change for societies which endure a season of distress and demise. Radical Islam is set to become a comprehensive ideology of mobilization, in the last phases of a conflict with the West.[32] However, Islam as such has proved unable to successfully tackle the substantive matters of development, democracy, and modernization.

1. Odd Arne Westad, *The Global Cold War. Third World Interventions and the Making of Our Times* (New York: Cambrige University Press, 2006).

2. D. F. Fleming, *The Cold War and its Origins,1917-1960* (London: G. Allen & Unwin, 1961).

3. Donald Levine, *Greater Ethiopia. The Evolution of a Multiethnic Society* (Chicago: University of Chicago Press 1974).

4. Christopher Clapham, *Africa and the International System. The Politics of State Survival* (Cambridge, UK: Cambridge University Press, 1996).

5. Bereket Habte Selassie, *Eritrea and the United Nations and Other Essays* (Trenton: The Red Sea Press, 1989).

6. Gian Paolo Calchi Novati, *Conflict and the Reshaping of States in the Horn of Africa*, in Alessandro Triulzi and Maria Cristina Ercolessi (eds.), *State, Power and New Political Actors in Postcolonial Africa*. (Milan: Feltrinelli, 2004).

7. Uoldelul Chelati Dirar and Gian Paolo Calchi Novati, "The Horn of Africa and Italy's Role: Forget Colonialism and Play Globalism", *Aleph*, No. 1, 2003, pp. 72-81.

8. John D. Hargreaves, *Decolonization in Africa* (London: Longman, 1996).

9. Stefano Poscia, *Eritrea, colonia tradita*. Rome: Edizioni Associate, 1989. Also Irma Taddia, *"At the Origin of the State/Nation Dilemma: Ethiopia, Eritrea and Ogaden in 1941,* Northeast African Studies, 12 (1990), No. 2-3, pp. 157-70.

10. Gian Paolo Calchi Novati, "Italy and the Triangle of the Horn: too Many Corners for a Half Power", *The Journal of Modern African Studies*, 32 (1994), No. 3, pp. 369-85.

11. Gian Paolo Calchi Novati, *Il Corno d'Africa nella storia e nella politica* (Turin: SEI, 1994).

12. Harold G.Marcus, *Ethiopia, the United States and the Soviet Union, 1941-1974* (Berkeley: University of California Press, 1983).

13. Tom J. Farer, *War Clouds on the Horn of Africa: The Widening Storm* (New York: Carnegie Endowment for International Peace, 1979). Also David A Korn, *Ethiopia, the United States and the Soviet Union* (Edwardsville: Carbondale, 1986).

14. Gian Paolo Calchi Novati, *Colonialism as State-Maker in the History of the Horn of Africa: A Reassessement*, in Svein Ege, Harald Aspen, Birhanu Teferra and Shiferaw Bekele (eds.), *Proceedings of the 16th International Conference of Ethiopian Studies* (Trondheim, 2009), pp. 233-44 (on line).

15. Alemseged Abbay, *Identity Jilted or Re-Imagining Identity? The Divergent Paths of the Eritrean and Tigrayan Nationalist Struggle.* (Lawrenceville/Asmara: The Red Sea Press, 1998); Lionel Cliffe and Basil Davidson (eds.), *The Long Struggle of Eritrea for Independence and Constructive Peace* (Nottingham: Spokesman, 1994), Jordan Gebre-Medhin, *Peasants and Nationalism in Eritrea* (Trenton: The Red Sea Press, 1989);

Yohannes Okbazghi, *Eritrea: a Pawn in World Politics* (Trenton: The Red Sea Press, 1991); Papstein, Robert, *Eritrea: Revolution at Dusk* (Trenton: The Red Sea Press, 1991); Roy Pateman, *Eritrea. Even the Stones Are Burning.* (Lawrenceville/Asmara: The Red Sea Press, 1998); David Pool, *From Guerrilla to Government. The Eritrean People's Liberation Front* (London: Currey, 2001); Redie Bereketeab, *Eritrea. The Making of a Nation, 1890-1991* (Uppsala: Uppsala University, 2000); Ruth Iyob, *The Eritrean Struggle for Independence: Domination, Resistance, Nationalism,1941-1993* (Cambridge, UK: Cambridge University Press, 1995); Medhanie Tesfatsion, *Eritrea. Dynamics of a National Question* (Amsterdam: Gruner, 1986).

16. Eyassu Gayim, *The Eritrean Question: the Conflict Between the Right of Self-Determination and the Interests of States* (Uppsala: Iustus Forlag, 1993).

17.Gian Paolo Calchi Novati, *Conflict and the Reshaping of States in the Horn of Africa*, in Alessandro Triulzi and Maria Cristina Ercolessi (eds.), *State, Power and New Political Actors in Postcolonial Africa* (Milan: Feltrinelli. 2004).

18. Daniel Volman, "Africa and the New World Order", *The Journal of Modern African Studies,* 31 (1993), No. 1, pp. 1-30.

19. Gian Paolo Calchi Novati, "L'imperatore e il presidente. Alle origini dell'alleanza tra Etiopia e Stati Uniti", *Africa* (Rome), 43 (1988), No. 3, pp. 360-77.

20. Bruno Loi, *Peace-keeping, pace o guerra? Una risposta italiana: l'operazione Ibis in Somalia* (Firenze: Vallecchi, 2004).

21. Walter S Clark and Jeffrey Herbst. *Learning from Somalia: The Lessons of Armed Humanitarian Intervention* (Boulder, Co.: Westview Press, 1997).

22. International Crisis Group, "Somalia. To Move beyond the Failed State": *Africa Report* (Brussel/Nairobi), No. 147, 2008.

23. Amare Tekle (ed.) *Eritrea and Ethiopia: From Conflict to Cooperation* (Lawrenceville/Asmara: The Red Sea Press, 1994).

24. John Abbink, , "Creating Borders: Exploring the Impact of the Ethio-Eritrean War on the Local Population.", *Africa* (Rome):56, (2001), No. 4, pp. 447-58.

25. Federica Guazzini, *Le ragioni di un confine coloniale. Eritrea 1898-1908* (Turin: L'Harmattan Italia, 1999).

26.·Gabriele Ciampi, "Cartographic Problems of the Eritreo-Ethiopian Border", *Africa* (Rome), 56 (2001), No. 2, pp. 155-89.

27. Uoldelul Chelati Dirar, "Etiopia-Eritrea: le ragioni di un conflitto annunciato", *Afriche e Orienti,* 1999, 2, pp. 13-20; Tekeste Negash and Kjetil Tronvoll *Brothers at War. Making Sense of the Eritrean- Ethiopian War* (Oxford: J. Currey, 2000).

28. Tesfatsion Medhanie, *Eritrea and Neighbours in the "New World Order". Geopolitics, Democracy and Islamic Fundamentalism* (Muenster: LIT, 1994).

29. Ruth Iyob. "The Ethiopian-Eritrean Conflict: Diasporic vs. Hegemonic States in the Horn of Africa, 1991-2000", *The Journal of Modern African Studies,* 38 (2000), No. 1, pp. 659-82.

30. Fabienne Le Houérou, *Ethiopie-Erythrée: frères ennemis de la Corne de l'Afrique* (Paris: L'Harmattan, 2000).

31. Andrea De Guttry, Harry G. Post and Gabriella Venturini (eds.) *The 1998-2000 War Between Eritrea and Ethiopia. An International Legal Perspective.* (The Hague: Asser Press, 2009).

32. Olivier Roy, *L'échec de l'Islam politique* (Paris: Seuil, 1992).

# Panel: The Security Issue
# and the Chances of Western Communism

## Liliana Saiu
### FINE, BUT LET US NOT RISK OVERVALUING THE ECONOMY

There is a tendency in Italy, no less than in many countries, to adopt an over-simplified view of the American political spectrum, and I am grateful to Gray for contributing to criticize it. On this, let me raise now a question about the 1970s again. Is it true that Watergate started an erosion of détente—that is, started killing détente? Perhaps the process started there, as disappointments related to Watergate made American liberals disillusioned and even disgusted about Nixon's policies as a whole. I also have some questions about D'Agata's paper. It was a very interesting one, and full of insights. Yet, I wonder whether we do not risk to overstretch the economic issues—particularly with regard to the relations between the United States and its allies—to the detriment of other important issues: security issues, for instance. Incidentally, I recall that "Security first" is just the title of one of the chapters in Willy Brandt's book entitled *Friedenspolitik*. Security is found as a main issue in every conversation, memorandum, and so on, which is related to relations between the United States and Italy during the 1970s. Italian governments, political scientists, and foreign policy officers, were literally terrified by a number of circumstances such as increased Soviet presence in the Mediterranean, possible domino effect of what had happened in Czechoslovakia in 1968, and then, after the elections in Chile, the fear of a sort of Chile effect in Italy. One of the main issues of the day was security, the reduction of US military forces in Italy, which was also associated with the problem of burden-sharing as regarded defense costs. Economic issues do not seem to affect the relationship to so wide an extent as D'Agata seems to suggest.

## Antonio Varsori
### NOR LET US RISK WISHFUL THINKING

I do not agree with some statements in D'Agata's paper. Everybody knows that Nixon and Kissinger were against the Italian Communist Party being a member of the Italian government. The question of the Italian Communist Party becoming a member of the government was an issue from about 1974 onward, and not before. Then you must remember what happened between 1974 and 1976 in other South Europeans countries: the revolution in Portugal; the end of the Colonels' regime in Greece; and later on, Franco's death. I can assure you that, from the records I saw, there was a deep divide between the policies pursued by Nixon and Kissinger until 1974 and the policy pursued by the Ford administration. Sure, Kissinger was still there; but the policy was completely different. It was a policy which gave up the idea of covert operations, it was a policy which stressed the importance of cooperation with other European major nations—in particular with France, Britain, and Western Germany. And the opinions of the cool West German social democrats, as well as of the British labor party government, were the same: that is, the communists must stay out of any Italian government.

In order to understand that, we should refrain from basing our interpretations on what happened, say, thirty years later—or on any sort of wishful thinking. Sure, in the mid-1970s, we Italians used to say something like "It's okay, Berlinguer is a good social democrat; okay, the Italian Communist Party is completely democratic, and so on, so there is no problem in their being a part of the Italian government". Though, we should not assume that everybody had the same idea.

If you take a look at the British records, as well as at other West European records, you see that their interpretation was completely different. In their opinion, the Communist party was not democratic. It was tied to "democratic centralism". Of course, the Italian communists were saying they were in favor of European integration and of NATO. But, following the interpretation of the American, British, German and French diplomats, that was not true. They used to say something like: "Okay, it may be; but, if the communists come to power, it's a threat not only to NATO but also to the European community. In that case, the future of Italy might be similar to what happened to Yugoslavia. But we don't like Yugoslavia; we can't accept one more Yugoslavia".

On the eve of the Italian general elections of 1976, during the Puerto Rico summit, and soon later during a secret meeting in Paris, it was not only the United States that supported the idea of doing something against the Italian Communists, but it was the French and the Germans. The Americans just aligned themselves. And it was no question of covert operations. Talk was about exploiting the economic instrument, of helping the Italian moderates—namely, Andreotti and the Christian Democrats—to avoid any presence of the communists in the government.

There was no idea of favoring the military or right-wing regimes either in Italy or in Spain or in Portugal. What was being reiterated, just as during the late 1940s and the 1950s, was: "We want democratic, anti-communist and anti-fascist regimes".

*Lawrence Gray*
AND WHAT IF ITALIAN COMMUNISM WAS UNDERVALUED?

I don't agree with you, Antonio, because the reasons why the Germans or the French were against communist power-sharing in Italy were not the same as those that motivated the Americans against the communists. When the French communists joined the French government as minor coalition partners in the early 1980s, reactions in Washington were something like '*Ma chi se ne frega!* Let them run the trains!'"

But when we come to the culture of Italian Communism we are talking about something qualitatively different. Italian communism developed on a different cultural and historical level. A quality gap is bridged when you come to the baggage that the PCI brought to the governing arena. Of course, democratic centralism was still there, the ties with Moscow were still there. But this was not the only issue. The real issue was what the rapprochement of that kind of party with the traditional governing elites would actually mean; what would it mean, what would be the result, and what would be the influence of the working relationship between a "serious" communist party with allied elites. Depending upon one's viewpoint this was both the fear and the promise of the *compromesso storico*. No one seemed to want Berlinguer's strategy at the time. But from today's perspective both followers and antagonists of the PCI of the 1970s may jointly conclude that it would have been better for the PCI to undergo change from an application of the *compromesso storico* strategy than undergo the inglorious demise it has experienced in recent years.

We should remember that the first thing that Kissinger said when he heard of the disturbances in Poland in 1980 was: "Good! That is really the last nail in the coffin of communism in the West, especially in Italy, because everyone will now focus on what the Soviets will do, and then it will be an issue of once again revealing the repressive side of communism". Kissinger welcomed social disturbances in Eastern Europe to counter the last vestiges of the electoral appeal of an "intelligent" communist party like the PCI.

Was there an alternative vision in dealing with a serious, social democratic oriented communist party like the PCI, a *sui generis* communist party within the European family of communist parties? I think this story is still incomplete, even with the remnants of the old PCI, within the brain trust of advisers who were working for the PCI, among those who were close to the party, allied with it, even among those within it.

Various strategies were proposed by American presidents from Nixon to Ford to Carter. But none of them represented an alternative and all remained committed to weaken the PCI by whatever means possible. All American Ambassadors during the 1970s and the 1980s were committed to isolating the PCI. One cannot find a more anti-communist American Ambassador to Rome than the one representing President Carter, the politically progressive Richard Gardner. Previous American Ambassadors to Italy were almost always involved in CIA operations. Gardner was supposed to be more open, he was advised by Brzezinski, yet even he was involved with CIA anti-communist maneuvers.

We must remember that Brzezinski, like Kissinger, was an intellectual from Europe. Today he may be a kind of grandfatherly highly informal adviser to Obama. He was very critical of the folly that the Bush administration has brought upon all of us during the past years. But he is from Eastern Europe; an intellectual who came from the periphery of the empire to its capital. He is conditioned by what needs to be done to run the Empire and he holds a high degree of anti-Russian skepticism.

Close to the highest levels of the leadership of the PCI during the 1970s and the 1980s was a small group of intellectuals whose central figure was Franco Rodano. This group was especially close to Berlinguer through the good offices of one of their own: Antonio Tatò, the chief of staff for Berlinguer and head of the PCI press office. The Rodano group shared a number of traits: Catholic, politically moderate, strategically pro-Soviet in a Rooseveltian manner; it is noteworthy that a small group, tightly knit, well organized and focused, can become highly influential if the group surrounds the right leader at the right time facing the right challenges.

*Varsori*—I wonder whether I was clear enough while making my remarks. I was not discussing the reality of the PCI, I was just discussing the perceptions and the analyses about the PCI. And as those analyses are concerned, Berlinguer was no problem, he was a nice gentleman. But that did not matter. They were communist. Nothing else mattered.

Of course, there was a difference in the strategy, particularly between the Nixon administration and the Carter administration. Nixon was ready for covert operations. He could think about Chile in1973. But there were differences in the American administration too. There were arguments between American ambassador Carlucci and Kissinger. Kissinger wanted to promote covert operations. Carlucci favored a more subtle strategy, looking for the right potential governing partners, and these were the socialist parties. By then, the situation was more complex. There were more actors. The Europeans—in particular the French and the Germans—wanted to play a major role, and the American administration was ready to give them some level of responsibility.

We cannot forget that 1974 and 1975 was a post-Watergate period, and the American administration was induced to prefer multilateral action rather than unilateral action—namely, acting together with the European allies. And the latter did not like covert action. They preferred other means, like moral suasion and some kinds of economic instruments.

Anyway, whatever was known about the different characters of the Italian communist party, Italy was seen as no exception within the framework of a more general problem, that is, the crisis of Southern Europe—Spain, Greece, Italy, and Turkey, and Cyprus. We must not forget that there was a whole Mediterranean area which was a part of the Atlantic alliance, and hence was important not only for the Americans, but was important also for the British, the Germans, and—to some extent—also for the French.

*Gray*—Let me recall something that may reinforce my point about risking an excessive emphasis on old parallel versions and analyses. We should remember that in 1974 Nagorsky, who worked for the Council on Foreign Relations, made a trip to Rome for private meetings with senior PCI leaders. In an interview with the press, following these meetings, Nagorski said: "Look, we'll give you (the PCI) everything you want. Do you want money? Do you want recognition? We'll do everything, but you have to change your name". Did they say that to anyone else? No, they said that only to the Italian Communist Party.

This may be viewed as a peculiarly American problem which is why apparently minor issues regarding names or labels can matter. There was a greater view of Europe—political, economic, security issues—that was important and to which most observers in the West subscribed, including Italian Communist leaders and American officials alike. But, for the Americans, the label "communism" was key and they would not budge on this issue. For the Americans, there could be no risk taken regarding the possibility, however remote, of seeing an authoritative PCI join a governing coalition and becoming a reference point for other leftist and progressive forces in Western Europe. Perhaps there could have been an alternative approach in dealing with the PCI, one that would have fit well with an earlier end to the Cold War. Indeed, with the help of hindsight, there is always an alternative vision available in political history. But the Americans were not capable at that historical moment of embracing any kind of alternative to their categorical opposition to communist parties coming to power in Western Europe.

## Raffaele D'Agata
### ON EUROPEAN LEADERSHIP AND ITALIAN COMMUNISTS

Let me wonder whether there ever was any general rule in Europe about not accepting you if you were named a communist whatever you did propose. In fact, early in 1968, a lot of trouble developed in West German politics when the press office of the Social Democratic Party issued a statement about the Italian Communist Party as a possible legitimate member of a Grand Coalition government in Italy according to the West German pattern of that time—that is, as the actual opposite number of the SPD itself. For about a week, that had a bombshell effect on both West German and Italian politics, until the leak was cautiously played down.

Anyway, Brandt's approach to the communist question was very peculiar. Let me also remember that just a little later, as Brandt was beginning his maneuvering out of the Grand Coalition government, and preparing the early election that would bring him to the Chancellorship, he managed to publish an interview with a popular Italian communist newspaper—which he prepared very carefully—where his open door to the Italian communist approach to European and international politics may sound really amazing if you read them today.

Of course, Brandt's attention to the PCI was also part of his search for convenient devices in order to ease the difficulties of his openings toward the Eastern bloc. But it may be observed that he still went on cultivating the Italian communist connection even after taking full control of policy after the elections of September 1969. Not until immediately after the Milan blast of December 1969, which opened the *strategia della tensione*—that is, the kind of permanent low-intensity covert action strategy which actually took place during the 1970s in order to contain the increase of left-wing influence in Italy and in Europe as a whole—did Brandt cautiously downgrade and virtually suspend his moves toward some deeper and more open understanding with the PCI. Indeed, Brandt knew very well that he was already having trouble enough to face if he was to pursue his policy without being overtly disavowed, not to say torpedoed, by the Nixon administration.

To finish, let me add some considerations about the relation between security stakes and economic stakes—both as regards international politics during the 1970s and in general. I simply wonder whether it is correct to see these two aspects as quite separated from each other. My question is: whenever security is claimed as a need, what is precisely meant to be kept safe? That question becomes more and more significant as more and more evidence is added about how US and Western top officials were quite aware from the very start that the Soviet leaders were not aiming at any kind of territorial expansion through military means, nor did they wish to see their own system being imitated too much, least of all in the West.

# The Contributors

*Gian Paolo Calchi Novati* is Professor of History and Institutions of African and Asian Countries at the University of Pavia and senior research fellow at the Istituto per gli Studi di Politica Internazionale (Milan). He is also a researcher at the Center for African Studies (Boston). Former Director of the Istituto per le Relazioni tra l'Italia e I Paesi dell'Africa, America Latina e Medio Oriente (IPALMO), his major publications include *La decolonizzazione* (Turin: Loescher, 1983), and *Africa: La storia ritrovata* (Rome: Carocci 2005) with Pierluigi Valsecchi.

*Raffaele D'Agata* is Professor of Contemporary History at the University of Sassari. He founded and edited the quarterly *Letture urbinati di politica e storia* (1998-2000) and has published books on international twentieth-century history, including *Da Monaco a Bretton Woods: l'evoluzione transnazionale degli interessi e degli scopi* (Milan: Franco Angeli, 1989) and *La nemesi dei prestadenaro:economia mondiale e Guerra fredda 1944-1948* (Soveria Manelli: Rubbettino, 2001).

*Lawrence Gray* is Professor of Political Science and International Relations at John Cabot University in Rome. A former Executive Director of the Commission for Cultural Exchange Between Italy and the United States (Fulbright), he is a partner of Surehand and Smith Gray LLC. His publications include *The Italian Communist Party: Yesterday, Today, and Tomorrow* (Greenwood Press, 1980) co-edited with Simon Serfaty; *Corporate Activities in the Era of Global Economy* (Tokyo: Keizai University Press, 1992); and *L'America di Roosevelt negli anni dell'esilio di Luigi Sturzo* (Soveria Mannelli: Rubbettino, 2002)

*Wilfried Loth* is Professor of Modern and Contemporary History (Chair) at the University of Duisburg-Essen (Germany) and Chairman of the EU Liaison Committee of Historians. He has published widely on European history, Catholicism, European integration and the Cold War. Major publications include, *The Division of the World, 1951-1955* (London/New York: Routledge 1987); *Stalin's Unwanted Child. The Soviet Union, the German Question, and the Foundation of the GDR* (London/New York: MacMillan 1998; and *Overcoming the Cold War. A History of Détente, 1950-1991* (Houndsmills/New York: Palgrave 2002)

*Rodolfo Ragionieri* has lectured on Mathematics for Social Sciences and Theories and Practices for Peace-keeping and Peace-building at the University of Florence. Currently he is Associate Professor of Political Science at the University of Sassari. A past chairman of the "Forum per i problemi della pace e della guerra" he is also member of the board of the Euroupean Peace Research Association. His books include *Identities and Conflicts: The Mediterranean* (Basingstoke: Palgrave,2001), and *Pace e guerra nelle relazioni internazionali* (Rome: Carocci, 2008)

*Liliana Saiu* is Professor of History of International Relations at Cagliari University, Sardinia, Italy. Her books include *The Great Powers and Rumania 1944-1946. A Study on the Early Cold War Era* (Boulder, Co.: East European Monographs, 1992) and *Stati Uniti e Italia nella Grande Guerra 1914-1918* (Florence: L.C. Olschki, 2003). She is presently working on Western Mediterranean security during the Cold War.

*Antonio Varsori* is Professor of History of International Relations and of History of European Integration at the University of Padua, where he is also the Director of the Department of International Studies. Member of the editorial boards of several journals, he is the editor of the series "Storia internazionale dell'età contemporanea", Franco Angeli (Milan) and co-editor of "Euroclio", PIE/Peter Lang (Brussels). Recent publications include *European Union History Themes and Debates*, ed. with W. Kaiser (Basingstoke: Palgrave, 2010).

*Odd Arne Westad* is Professor of International History at the London School of Economics and Political Science (LSE) and Co-Director of LSE Ideas (previously known as Cold War Studies Centre (CWSC) with Michael Cox. He was the International Co-ordinator of the Russian Foreign Ministry's Advisory Group on Declassification and Archival Access, and the author of many books, including *The Global Cold War: Third World Interventions and the Making of Our Time* (winner of the the 2006 Bancroft Prize and the Akira Iriye International History Book Award). Founding editor of the journal *Cold War History* and co-editor of the three-volume *Cambridge History of the Cold War*.

www.ingramcontent.com/pod-product-compliance
Lightning Source LLC
Chambersburg PA
CBHW021822270326
41932CB00007B/291